PRAISE FOR
JIMMY "SUPERFLY" SNUKA

"The Jimmy Snuka legacy will always be not what he did in the ring but what he did above the ring. His body splash off the top of a steel cage is the most impressive move I've ever seen. It was his signature. Others tried it. Mick Foley. Shawn Michaels. Even Hulk Hogan tried to splash the Big Boss Man from the top of the cage. But nobody—and I mean nobody—could do it as gracefully and effectively as Jimmy 'Superfly' Snuka."

—Mean Gene Okerlund, WWE announcer and Hall of Famer

"I can't say Jimmy Snuka is the best of all time, but he was the best of *his* time. At that point, wrestling needed somebody like him, and what he brought to the table was blowing fans' minds. He wasn't a rushed wrestler. He took his time, but he knew when to do the high-flying spots. There has never been anybody like him. The Jeff Hardys and RVDs are awesome wrestlers, but there will never be another Jimmy Snuka. He's one of a kind."

—Kurt Angle, Impact Wrestling and
former WWE star and Olympic gold-medalist

"I was senior editor and photo editor at a pro wrestling magazine when I first saw him. I hadn't seen him in person, but when I saw a picture of him in midair, high above the ring in a match against 'Alaskan' Jay York, I was amazed. I had never seen anyone like this. We started running stories on him right away. When I did meet him in New York, he was always grateful we ran a story. He sold magazines whenever we put him on the cover."

—Bill Apter, wrestling journalist

"Jimmy was the only guy in the business who could watch someone do something in the ring and then be able to go out there and do the same thing."

—*Matt Borne, the original Doink the Clown*

"Everyone would talk about Jimmy's great athletic ability, but workers within the industry always knew what a great wrestler he was. He was a great draw wherever he went, whether he was a babyface or a heel. I was fortunate to grow up in New York, and I paid a lot of money to see Jimmy Snuka on the card."

—*Tommy Dreamer, former ECW, WWE, and TNA Wrestling star*

"Look where he's from, and look where he ended up. He was one of the best workers in the business, and he did it the old-fashioned way: he earned it. Nothing was given to him. He made his own legacy."

—*Paul Orndorff, WWE Hall of Famer*

"When Jimmy Snuka jumped off the cage, it made me do what I want to do. I was a daredevil. I didn't do any cliff jumping, but in elementary school, I would always jump from the highest limb on the tree. Snuka started all of that, and I can't thank him enough. He started something, and I've made my living off of it."

—*Jeff Hardy, TNA and former WWE star*

"I remember seeing Jimmy Snuka in his prime. He was my favorite wrestler when I was a kid.... He's the kind of guy who, if you saw him at a bar, you'd just be like, 'Hey Jimmy!' He's got that vibe. There are not a lot of guys who were like that. He had this earthy quality to him that's so rare, and certainly fans connected with that."

—Billy Corgan, Smashing Pumpkins founder/lead singer and
RESISTANCE Pro Wrestling creative director

"He had a mystery about him...well, it seemed that way when I was 10. We, of course, used to imitate him and his signature move from the top rope. I remember him being a 'good guy' but you almost never knew what he was gonna do."

—Constantine Maroulis, Tony-nominated
Broadway star and American Idol finalist

"My brother and I watched Jimmy Snuka wrestle on TV in North Carolina in the 1970s, and we were obsessed with him. When he would climb up to the top rope, we would howl, 'From the top rope...' And then when he launched himself into the air like a muscle-bound bat and crush some villainous opponent, we'd scream, 'Superfly!' Then we'd pull old mattresses into the backyard and have neighborhood smackdowns."

—Clark Gregg, co-star of Iron Man, Thor, and The Avengers

SUPERFLY
The Jimmy Snuka Story

JIMMY SNUKA
WITH JON CHATTMAN

TRIUMPH
B O O K S

Library of Congress Cataloging-in-Publication Data
Snuka, Jimmy, 1943–
  Superfly : the Jimmy Snuka story / Jimmy Snuka with Jon Chattman.
    p. cm.
  ISBN 978-1-60078-758-4 (hardback)
  1. Snuka, Jimmy, 1943- 2. Wrestlers—Fiji—Biography. 3. Wrestlers—United States—Biography. I. Chattman, Jon. II. Title.
  GV1196.S68 2012
  796.812092—dc23
  [B]
                    2012027034

This book is available in quantity at special discounts for your group or organization. For further information, contact:

Triumph Books LLC
814 North Franklin Street
Chicago, Illinois 60610
(312) 337-0747
www.triumphbooks.com

Printed in U.S.A.

ISBN: 978-1-60078-758-4

Design by Amy Carter

Photos courtesy of the author and WWE unless otherwise indicated

I WOULD LIKE TO DEDICATE THIS BOOK TO
MY BEAUTIFUL ANGEL, MY WIFE, MY EVERYTHING

CONTENTS

FOREWORD

I met Jimmy Snuka back in Portland, but we only became close many years later. I was a rookie at the time, and he was about to leave. We would meet up again down the road and become brothers. Jimmy had gotten his big break in Portland, and they just loved him there. If that place could sing…holy cow! Jimmy learned how to wrestle and expanded on everything he was taught. The package was already put together by the time he debuted in Portland—the look and everything.

He wore the lei and seashells around his neck because he knew where he came from. This was a man who danced on fire and dove off cliffs. With his island look, he was like a real-life Tarzan. Leap-frogging off the top of the rope was nothing for him. It was like taking a step off the curb is for the rest of us.

Jimmy always studied everything and made it his own. Wrestling was the Wild West back then, not what it is today. Jimmy was going pretty hard, and when we were in Charlotte we would bang out seven or eight towns a week. It was a brutal territory. All the bruddas, as Jimmy would say, would do 90 interviews each Tuesday there. We'd be running in all these towns, and all of us would have to do these interviews for each market, and each one had to be different. So, here's Jimmy with Dusty Rhodes, Ric Flair, Andre the Giant, the Briscos, and Jimmy Valiant, and those guys were pretty good on the mic. But even with his limited vocabulary, Jimmy was able to get over using his eyes and his emotions. It wasn't what he said; the whole magic of Jimmy was his heart and his soul. That's why cameramen needed to zoom in on his eyes during promos. For Jimmy, it was all in the eyes. His eyes are the window to his soul. And when he goes out there, Jimmy opens up his soul. When he was in the Carolinas, he and Ricky "The Dragon" Steamboat had so many classic matches. Jimmy had a lot of classic matches with a lot of guys—he just went so hard in that territory and really came into his own.

By the time Jimmy got to New York, he was on fire. He was primed and ready. He was rolling with the big dogs and drawing a lot of money. But they did a dirty thing to him: they made him a heel. They tried him as a bad guy, but the fans just loved him anyway. Jimmy was getting over so much that a guy who came into New York got angry when he couldn't get over Jimmy.

When Hulk Hogan came in, Jimmy and Don Muraco had been carrying the entire New York territory. When they put Jimmy in a cage match against Muraco....holy cow! It was amazing when Jimmy climbed up where no one dared to go. What a moment that was. When he looked at Muraco and brought those hands up, the flashbulbs went off. Muraco was lying on his back, and Jimmy didn't just dive off. He did a half-squat and swandove out there. He gave Muraco the charley horse of a lifetime. Muraco won the match, but that was done on purpose. There was no underhandedness on Muraco's part at all. That was done to make room for someone new.

I was the one Jimmy feuded with next. As a heel, working

with someone like Jimmy is a dream. The Piper's Pit we made almost instantly brought wrestling into a new age. Everybody was just like, "What just happened?" After it aired, it was like a bomb went off. It was hard to get around. I thought people were going to stab me after I hit him with the coconut. I'd been stabbed before.

I love Jimmy, but the reason I brought in the coconuts, bananas, and pineapples was he only could say, like, three words. This was the second time I had him on the Pit, and he wouldn't talk. The first time, he didn't talk, and the second time, we just stared at each other. I was like, "Oh man, I've got two minutes and 54 seconds and this guy is not going to say anything. What am I going to do?" So, I just asked him to get me something from Fiji, and two hours later, we filmed it again. I was trying to figure out what to do. I don't know how many guys would've stood for that.

I don't think I'd ever had a coconut in my hand before that day. It just came up when a coconut dropped out of a paper bag. There were six or seven coconuts in there, and I'm trying to fill the three minutes we had but I had nothing to say. I was looking at Jimmy as if to say, "Are you sure about this?" He told me to hit him with it. He didn't run over in slow motion and say, "Yeah, let's do that." It was an idea, and in my mind, he had given me permission. I wouldn't have done it otherwise.

People have called it the greatest angle in the history of professional wrestling. There have been a lot of great angles, but this one is hard to beat. I do think it took something out of Jimmy. I don't know. I was wrestling him every night to big crowds. There was tension there all the time because of what I did on TV. We got into it in Chicago in a hotel hallway one night, but I was not mad at him. It took me a while to realize it, but he sacrificed his whole career for me. What do I say about a man who did that? From there, we became brothers, and I started watching out for him.

I think Jimmy's career was cut short in the WWF. I feel there were four or five years where he could have been on top. After he was in Hogan's corner at the first WrestleMania, something snapped with Jimmy. He just left. It was a brutal, vicious business back then, and Jimmy was hurt by it. There was a lot of pressure on a guy who didn't really know who to trust, and he was always dependent on somebody else because English isn't his first language. He hooked up with some wicked white people. He was trained under territorial rules, and all of a sudden there was a new world order in New York, and there were no rules.

I'm proud any time someone mentions my name alongside Jimmy "Superfly" Snuka's name. He's perfect in every way. The best word to describe him is *organic*. Everything about Jimmy is so real; his words in this book are no different. It's Jimmy—laying his soul on the line, for the fans, just like he always has.

—Rowdy Roddy Piper

INTRODUCTION

During my senior year of high school, it was not uncommon for me to stay home to watch Jimmy Snuka wrestle. Sure, my social calendar wasn't that full, but I remember being invited to parties and telling people "no" because I was watching Jimmy Snuka that night. He had that big an effect on me. I think I got to touch him in 1980 in Syracuse, and I thought my life had just peaked. You couldn't go to an acting class and say here's the "Snuka look" and perfect it. An Oscar winner couldn't do it. To take 20,000 people and make them simultaneously feel something inside is a gift that not many people in entertainment have. Snuka was able to convey this. He kept people emotionally captivated in his matches.

A couple months before that infamous cage match in 1983, I attended my first live wrestling show at Madison Square Garden. I watched the first match in the Don Muraco/Jimmy Snuka trilogy. I just remember Jimmy's great words: "I'm not through with you yet, Don Muraco." I was glued. And that cage match with Muraco, which I write about in my own autobiography, was the moment I really felt like I wanted to make people feel the way Snuka had made me feel.

It was such an emotional moment. It was a moment in time. It took everything else Snuka had done to get him to the top of the cage. It was all those road trips in Japan, breaking in and doing time in the Carolinas and Portland. Everything led to that moment. It was so much more than just the athletic feat of reaching the top of the cage. It was the anticipation of it, his timing, and the spectacle of it all—his slinging his hair back, putting up the "I love you" sign, and launching into the air.

I've always been fascinated with moments in time that people are remembered for. Sometimes it's the worst moments in their lives that are remembered, but in Jimmy's case, everything he had done before and after was going to pale in comparison to that one moment in time.

In 1990, Jimmy and I had a lumberjack match in front of 300 or 400 fans in a 17,000-seat arena in Las Vegas, and it was far from a classic match. It was completely improvised, and we ended up doing a double count-out, and that never happens. I remember being given the task of telling Jimmy the outcome, which was not supposed to be in his favor. I guess he wasn't happy with that so I came up with a double count-out. That's not supposed to happen—you actually have lumberjacks there *specifically* so you don't leave the ring area. It was ludicrous. I'm sure it wasn't memorable for Jimmy, but for me, to wrestle the guy who had been my biggest inspiration, it was a big match. I was nervous, but at the same time I felt confident. I had some national TV exposure and was determined to make it a good match. After all, I was out there in the ring with my hero.

I believe Jimmy was taken away from WWF fans too soon. I went to the Garden to see him against Rowdy Roddy Piper, and didn't see him again for a while. I know he resurfaced in the AWA and later in WWF again, but I feel kind of cheated in regard to the magic of the Snuka era. I still have the Superfly poster that hung over my bed during my senior year of high school and freshman year in college.

To make a baseball comparison, it was like when Ted Williams was taken away from the Red Sox during World War II—but at least there was a more logical reason for Ted's absence. We missed out on what would've been the best run of Jimmy's career. Everybody who meets Jimmy knows he has some human frailties, but that's real life. Just because you can have 20,000 people in the palm of your hand doesn't means you can control your life any better than the rest of us. All you can ask for is kindness and decency in your heroes. Jimmy has not disappointed me yet.

—Mick Foley

PREFACE

The word *fear* is not a part of my vocabulary. This brudda doesn't
know what that word means. I never have and I never will. It
has no meaning to me. Growing up in the Fiji Islands, the Gilbert
and Marshall Islands, and eventually Hawaii, I was never afraid
of anything. Danger means nothing to the Superfly. I live my
life to the max without giving much thought to how dangerous
something can be or how impossible it might be. I make the impossible possible—I always have, long before I jumped off the
top of the steel cage at Madison Square Garden.

Heights mean nothing to this brudda, either. I can't tell you
how many times I used to dive off cliffs as a kid. I loved birds.
I'd always look up to the sky, and I was fascinated with them.
I wanted to know how it felt to fly. I remember when my children were born, I thought about getting wings tattooed on my
back. It seemed right. A lot of natives from the islands get tattoos, and I wanted it to look like I really could fly. But I never
went through with it. My children didn't want to see me get tattoos. They didn't like it so I never got it, but it doesn't matter.

The Superfly doesn't need tattoos to prove he can fly. My
whole career I've soared like an eagle, brah! As a kid I would

dive off boats and cliffs and yell "Superfly!" That's how I got my name. It was only natural that when I needed a gimmick as a wrestler, I used something from my childhood.

I wasn't only fascinated with flying, brah. I wanted to swing tree to tree, just like my idol, Tarzan. I remember in Fiji, my mother, Louisa, would take my brother, Henry, and me to the movies to watch Tarzan, and I wanted to be just like him. Oh man, I loved that guy right away. I remember telling her, "I want to be like that man." When you see me in the ring today or on video, you'll notice I always wear a headband and leopard print as a tribute of sorts to Tarzan. I often wore shells around my neck as a tribute to my culture. I also went barefoot, just like he did. I admit, though, that I didn't wear boots in the ring partly because no one from the islands wants their toes to be trapped in a pair of anything other than flip-flops, brudda!

In many ways, I'm a real-life Tarzan. I never stopped swinging from trees. When I got into the wrestling ring, I'd swing rope-to-rope and perch myself on top, just as I did as a kid on those cliffs. Everything just came natural to this brudda. I was an explorer and the islands were my playground, my education… my everything.

Like Tarzan, I never could sit still. I always need to be moving, and I need to be in the ring locking up with somebody and feeling the energy of the crowd. I love the fans. Everything I've ever done is for them. That's what makes my life these days so hard and extremely frustrating. I'm writing this just a week or so after having had major reconstructive ankle surgery. The Superfly isn't in the ring. Instead, he's in a recliner for the next six weeks with his ankle high in the air. This is going to be the hardest thing I have ever done. Even worse, I will not be able to get back in the ring for six months after that, at least. But I had to have the surgery. It was a hard decision to get it done, but I have been pretending my ankle hasn't been bothering me for the last 30 years, brah!

I spent years taping up my ankle, through torn ligaments and complete tears, because when I wrestled, I didn't feel anything. I might've been in agony every time I was outside the ring, but once I was inside it, forget it, brah. It just felt fine. I was in my element. For so many years, I was numb to it. Feeding off my fans made all the pain go away. But as I've gotten older and matches have gotten fewer and fewer over the years, the pain caught up with the Superfly.

I can honestly say I haven't been 100 percent for ring action for many years. Like I said, I masked the pain. I tried not to see how swollen my ankle was after each show. I pretended everything was okay, and that it didn't bother me. I ignored the pain. Each time I'd work an independent show and couldn't get to the top rope to do my signature Superfly leap, it reminded me how hurt I really was. There were way too many times I had to do it from the second rope, or worse, the first rope. I didn't like that. My wife, Carole, told me fans didn't notice, but I knew they did. That's what they came for—to watch me fly!

I'm 68 years old as I write this, but all this pain has had nothing to do with getting older. Yes, maybe the years took their toll on my ankle, but never my ability. If my ankle was 100 percent, I know I'd be able to jump off the top rope for sure. If I hadn't abused my ankle for all these years, I know I could have done any show from the top rope. Actually, the third rope would be too low—I know I could still get to the top of the cage. But I never wanted surgery because I never wanted to be without wrestling. I always needed to be in the ring. That's my home.

I finally realized I needed surgery on November 11, 2011.

That day, I had been with longtime friend Dawn Marie, who I helped break into the business, for a New York City Veteran's Day Parade. After the parade we had to walk four blocks to get to the bus to bring us home. I could barely move, and they had to flag a car down to drive me those four city blocks. I'd been limping around for a while, but in that moment even I realized I couldn't deny it anymore.

> **"He was in so much pain. Every step he took was just this excruciating pain. You could see it on his face."**
> —Dawn Marie, former WWE Diva and ECW star

So, a few weeks later I set up the surgery, and I went into the Jefferson University Hospital and got it done. Now, I'm keeping my foot elevated and letting this ankle heal. I'm already feeling better, but I miss being in the ring. That's what I love. That's what I'm here to do. I'm supposed to be resting and out of the ring for a long time, but I know I'll be back doing what I do best. I remember telling my doctors I'd be back in the ring again flying high, and they couldn't believe it. They don't know me. Carole does, and she doesn't think I'll be able to hold out for the full six months. She's probably right. I love entertaining the fans, watching their faces, and seeing them have fun. I enjoy the friendship I have with the boys. They're like my family when I am on the road.

The way I live my life is, I want what I want, when I want it, brudda. And being strapped in this big chair sitting on my ass and healing is not what the Superfly wants. All that runs through my mind is the past and the future. I love what I've done, and

I want to do more. As I sit here, I remember all that I've accomplished in my career and personal life, and I want more of those moments.

Sometimes being trapped with my thoughts can be more painful than any injury I've suffered in the ring. But as I look back, I can also look ahead, and that takes the sting away. Anything I've ever wanted in my life—whether it was using the Fiji Islands as my playground or learning the wrestling business in Portland, Oregon—I've had to figure out on my own and bust my ass to own it. I'm not ready to change that mind-set. What this time has made me remember is all the things I've done—my highs, my lows, my failures, and my regrets.

CHAPTER 1

A REAL-LIFE TARZAN

"Jimmy was just always outside—a social animal.
When we had firewalkers come through—they came to the
University of Hawaii—Jimmy wanted to be with them
and get on their program. All of a sudden, there was
Jimmy walking on hot coals with the firewalkers.
I was impressed. We always were. He was grander than life.
That was his thing. He'd just step out and do things
that were extraordinary to common folk."
—Louise Reiher, Jimmy's sister

Bula bula vinaka! That means "hello" in my native language of Fijian, and I've never forgotten my roots. I was born James Wiley Smith in the Fiji Islands, or Viti, as we call it, on May 18, 1943. I have deep roots in the Fiji Islands. My mother, Louisa Vitu Smith, was the youngest of 12 children. The father of my great-grandmother, "Adi from Bua" (meaning Fijian princess), was a signer of the Deed of Cession in 1876.

I was the result of a love affair between my mother and a man she met named Charles Wimbledon Benjamin Thomas, who had

worked in Majesty-navy customs. I never knew this man as a child. He could not marry my mother, because he was already married and she was arranged to be married to someone else. Despite being four months pregnant with me, she married an engineer by the name of Bernard Reiher. He was contracted to work for the navy, so he was often away from home.

I was named after my mother's dad, Captain James Wiley Smith. Captain Smith and Bernie's father, Captain Adolph Reiher, did not get along with each other. I've heard the two of them were business rivals—blackbirders, which meant they fooled people into working for them as laborers. My grandfather actually transported slaves from Tasmania.

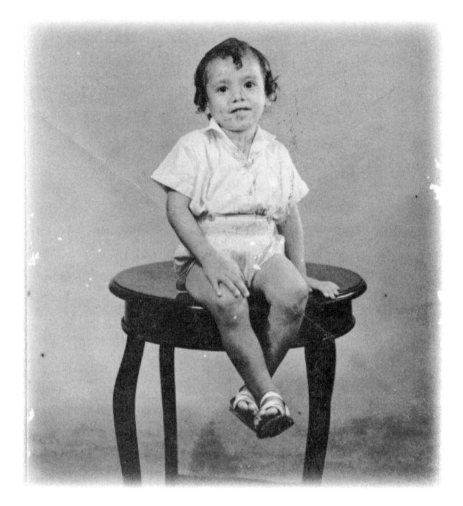

Since my mother was pregnant, Captain Reiher didn't want her to marry into the family, but he eventually agreed to it. I think I ended up paying the price for this. Everything about my early years was confusing. Every time I got used to something, it changed on me and threw me for a loop. My grandmother, Losana, took care of me. We all lived in a big house up in the hills of Suva. It was me, my mom, my stepfather, my grandmother, my uncles, and their families.

My younger brother, Henry Reiher, was born three years later, in 1946. Because Henry was his biological son, Bernie always treated him better than me. My mom took care of Henry a lot when he was young; I know my mom loved me, but I was with my grandmother a lot of the time. She gave me baths, dressed me, and let me sleep in her bed. Because of this, I thought for a while that my grandmother was actually my mother, and my mother was my aunt or something. I was too young to understand. It was not until my mother, stepbrother, stepdad, and I left for the Gilbert Islands when I was seven years old that I found out the truth. After learning my grandmother was staying in the Fiji Islands, I cried out because I didn't want to leave my mother. My real mom said to me, "I'm your mother." It blew my mind, brudda!

NEXT STOP: THE GILBERT ISLANDS

Bernie had to move away for work, so we went to the Gilbert Islands from Fiji with a plan to eventually settle in the Marshall Islands, where my stepfather's family was from. Since it took time for boats to reach us, my stepfather and mother knew we would be in the Gilberts for a while. Life got even more confusing while we waited on the dock the day we were scheduled to leave. I was playing around with Henry one day when all of a sudden, a man in uniform who worked for Her Majesty's Customs Department came up to

My biological father, Benjamin Thomas

me and said, "Hello, my son." I didn't realize at that moment that he was my real father. I just thought, *Who is this big, tall man calling me "son"?* When I was a teenager, I found out that this man was my real father. But I'll tell you more about that later, brudda.

My mother, Louisa

When we moved to the Gilberts, we lived in a big hut that the military built for the men who were stationed there. Life there wasn't like it was in the United States, that's for sure. We didn't have electricity, for example, so we had to carry a lantern. My mother cooked on a wood-fired stove. We ate fresh food every day. I would help my mother by going to buy a loaf of bread in the morning at one of the little local stores. It was made fresh every day and smelled so good. I remember walking home with the bread and picking the edges apart and eating them. By the time I got to the house, I had eaten both ends of the loaf.

We got our milk from the can or drank coconut milk. We had a line of credit at the store that my stepdad would pay off at the end of the week. We also had our own chickens and pigs that we ate. It was my job to kill the chickens. I'd just swing them around by their necks and they would run around until they dropped. Then, I'd chop their heads off and boil them for soup. We ate the feet. We didn't waste a thing. I was a regular jungle man. We made spears out of the bones and used the feathers for fishing. Island people don't waste anything, brudda!

My mom worked very hard—she did so many chores and really helped us kids out by watching over us and keeping us in check. She and my stepdad slept in one room and the kids were all in the other. It couldn't have been easy taking care of all of us—especially me, since I was probably a pain in the ass. My mom did it all.

TOUGH TIMES IN EBI

Living in the islands presented unique challenges. If you want to go someplace in New York, for example, you just get in a cab or take a bus or even a train. But in the islands, brudda, getting around wasn't as easy. There is water everywhere, and it wasn't like you could just get up and go places. All the islands, like Fiji and the Marshall Islands, were made up of smaller islands within them. Sometimes it took years to get a boat to take us between the islands. That was the case in going from the Gilbert Islands to the Marshall Islands.

When we got to Ebi, we lived in a small house I built with my brother and stepfather. Like my natural ability to play sports, I was pretty skilled at putting things together with my hands. The Reihers were a very respected family there, so my stepfather was able to get land to build a home. We started out with a generator but eventually got electric power in the house. I remember we had this huge tank in the backyard for water, and the military would bring water to us each day when we ran out.

My mom and dad were close, even though he hit her around a bit. Henry and I would see them kiss every morning and night. But my stepfather grew more strict and more angry once we arrived in the Marshalls. He'd drink a lot and he'd beat up on us good—me especially. He would assign Henry and me chores each day, but I would lose track of time playing around and end up not doing them. My stepfather would beat me because I always skipped out on work. Each time he did, my mom would just sit and cry. She couldn't do anything about it. Anytime she spoke out, he'd hit her, too.

> "I remember seeing my father take a 2x4 to both Henry and Jimmy. He was a strict man. All the people on the island said his own father was like that and that his grandfather was, too. If you didn't walk the line the way he wanted you to, you'd suffer the consequences."
> —Louise Reiher

I remember trying to talk Henry into running away with me many times because I wanted to explore the islands and didn't want to get beat. Sometimes we tried to leave—he often followed me everywhere I went, but when we were found, I was always the one who got beat. One day Henry and I were hiding from my stepfather because we knew we were going to get a beating. I told Henry I would take him home, but I was going to go back out because I knew I was going to get a beating. Henry stayed with me and we hid inside a boat along the beach...and then we felt water. My stepfather had found us and was throwing water on the boat to force us out. We were soaking wet when he brought us home. How far can you go on an island, brudda? When we got home, Henry and I got beat. I got the worst of it because my stepfather said I was a bad influence.

"He was the kind of guy who didn't like staying home. He got me in trouble a time or two. He was always into mischief. Being the younger brother, I picked up the slack when Jimmy wasn't around. Eventually I got tired of those beatings and just said, 'No, man, I ain't going' when Jimmy wanted to go out."
—Henry Reiher, Jimmy's brother

I was too much for my stepfather and mother to handle. When we moved to the Marshalls and my sisters Agnes, Louise, and Vicky were born, it was just too much for my mom and especially my stepfather, who had had enough of me.

My mom would take a ship back to the Fiji Islands to give birth and then spend a couple of months there to be with her family. She would take the babies back with her each time, so she had the three girls in Fiji. The first time she left for Fiji, Henry and I were put on a ship to Pohnpei for boarding school. She found out how to speak Gilberto and Marshallese in that time, while Henry and I learned to speak Ponapean. Henry and I used to speak in that language when we got back, just to irritate our parents. It really pissed Bernie off. My mom would laugh, and he didn't like it.

I will admit that I was a mischievous kid. I was at a Catholic boarding school, Christ the King, in Kolonia, Pohnpei, for three years because I was too much for my stepfather and mother to handle. They sent Henry with me, and I tried to take care of him. We were the new kids, and older kids would want to fight us. I tried to stay out of it, but it was hard. The school was on a plantation and the boys all worked the field. We would get up early to go to Mass, then have tea and bread for breakfast before going to class. After school, we would work in the field planting sweet potatoes, bananas, and more. We raised pigs, cows, and goats. Each

My brother, Henry, my mother, Louisa, and my sisters (left to right) Vicky, Louise, and Agnes

night was the same. We would eat dinner (usually the chicken or pig that was raised there), and we would do our homework. We got to play a little on the weekends—I remember playing soccer and baseball. I also ran track there. I did that at the Marshalls, too. I was very fast, and back in the Marshall Islands, I'd always win contests. The prize was always candy, which I gave to my sister Vicky.

It was hard because Henry and I wouldn't see our family for two years. We only saw them in our third year during summer vacation. I remember spending Christmases at the school when all the other kids went home to see their families. It was sad. The place was so empty. We had no phones and no way to travel home.

I remember learning how to play the tuba in school, and that was cool. I played it in the marching band, while Henry played sax. I remember one day we were waiting for a boat—the band would play to welcome people off the boat—and Henry dropped his mouthpiece into the water. I dove into the water between the pier and the boat to get it. I was not afraid, but Henry was. Henry didn't like the water as much as I did. I remember trying to teach him how to dive, but he couldn't. Later, I'd surf Sunset Beach in Hawaii on the North Shore specifically because they had the biggest waves anywhere.

I'd rather be in the ocean than anywhere else, brah. I never

The bell tower at Christ the King

liked school, so I acted out a lot. I was the ringleader who would convince my friends to go out late and surf. I was a bad boy. I got beat in school by the teachers just like I did at home, but I was smart. I might not have been book smart, but the Superfly always learns from his experiences. I would always pad my back with something, knowing full well they would hit me in the same spot on my back. You catch on when you're a rascal like I was.

We got beat a lot of times because of those fights I mentioned. There was a worker who would watch the boys fight and then would break it up after a while. Eventually, our parents brought us home. I stopped playing tuba—that's for sure. That was school property.

> "The first boarding school we went to was next to a bell tower. It was a really dangerous building built by the Spaniards right after the Spanish-American War. It was the only thing left standing—everything else had been bombed or crumbled. The stairs that went up to the bells were gone, but there were wooden ladders in their place that you could climb up. Mostly older kids were assigned to ring it because it was such a big bell. Little guys like us would just literally hang from the rope and hardly move it."
> —Henry Reiher

My parents sent us to another boarding school, Assumption, for three years or so in Majuro in the Marshall Islands—again not seeing much of my family. There was one building for the school, and the boys helped build a dormitory out of brick and mortar. They also built the girls dormitory and a convent for the nuns. While we were there, we figured out how to cook and how to wash and iron our own uniforms. The school was by the ocean, and we would all fish for food. I was used to that already. Some boys would take the net out and hold it as the other boys pounded on the water and chased the fish into the nets. The boys would carry big bags over their shoulders and fill it with fish for the month.

One day, I was surfing and saw a little girl being swallowed up by the waves. I dove in and dragged her out of the ocean. Her family invited me to their home for dinner. I remember thinking how nice it was to have a home-cooked meal. I had resented my family for sending me away, but I understood why they did it. I don't think of myself as a hero. I never have. This brudda just does what he does without thinking too much about it. Just like climbing that steel cage at Madison Square Garden, I just dove in the water to help that girl without giving it much thought. I love everybody, brudda. I didn't want to see that girl hurt.

READING AND WRITING IN ENGLISH

It's hard for me to say this, but the years I spent at boarding school and at a church near my house were the only years I ever spent in a classroom. It was always a challenge for me to stay focused enough to learn. Some days they would take us outside and we would sit under a tree as the nuns read us stories. But I was never good at reading. If I was not good at something, I didn't want to do it. I'm good at math, but reading and writing and spelling were like poison to me.

When I left the Fiji Islands and moved to the Gilbert Islands, I only spoke the Fijian pidgin language. They spoke some English in the Gilbert Islands, so I had to learn by listening to it. That helped me communicate a little, but I never figured out to read or write in English. My mother tried to help me learn, but I was stubborn and wanted nothing of it. She probably got tired of me not wanting any part of it. She was a very strong-willed and high-spirited person, but I guess I was just too much to handle.

I may not be able to read or write, but I can speak many languages. When I'm in Japan, I speak Japanese, for example. I learn by ear all the time. My whole life, brudda, I listened to the grown-ups and always asked questions. I still can't grasp the English language fully. That's why some of my promos might not have made 100 percent sense to you, but in my mind, I made sense. I still feel that way.

One of my most memorable sayings, "TV wonderland," actually came about by mistake. I was doing an on-camera promo and I wanted to say hello to everyone all over the world. I was thinking about how wonderful it was that I could talk to people from every land. It came out wrong though—I said I wanted to talk to all the people out there in "TV wonderland." People still dig when I say that.

> "Jimmy had very broken English but he managed to make it through. I had to do an interview with him in early 1985 for WrestleMania I. Vince McMahon was there working with the talent, and we were having problems getting what we needed out of Jimmy. Eighteen takes and an hour and a half later, we got by. He had many problems early on in expressing himself, but the fans always got the message."
> —Mean Gene Okerlund, WWE announcer and Hall of Famer

"In a business that is all about promos, it says a lot that Jimmy got as far as he did without being a great promo guy. He wasn't just a good worker—there are a million good workers—it was his athletic ability. With his promos, there was another side to him. The island thing made him different. People didn't know what to make of him. There was an element of danger with Jimmy, and if he flipped the switch, he was scary."
—Dave Meltzer, creator of the Wrestling Observer Newsletter

I don't prepare anything before I go on the microphone. The words just come to me then and there. I am not an educated guy—I don't always understand the big words, so I would just say whatever I wanted. I don't get nervous. I'm having fun. When the camera turns on, I turn on. I think that if fans take the time to listen to what I'm saying, they would understand me. The people that don't understand me are the people who are not listening. I might not use the right words all the time—my wife likes to talk about the time I called someone "constipated" instead of "complicated"—but I know it didn't matter because the passion was there.

You know what, brudda? I just let my eyes tell the story. I like doing promos.

"I remember one time his promo went for almost 23 minutes. He was talking about being from the islands, being near a volcano, how it erupted, and there were no boats. I just remember wondering, *What is this man talking about?* It didn't matter. Whatever he said, he delivered with such passion. You just looked into his eyes and you were like, 'Holy crap, this person wants to kill you.'"
—Tommy Dreamer, former ECW, WWE, and TNA star

I remember one night while living in the Gilbert Islands, I ate dog food. I thought it was corned beef hash or something. What did I know? I couldn't read the label. That was embarrassing, but it couldn't have been that bad because I ate the whole can, brudda! On a serious note, I know I was taken advantage of throughout my wrestling career because of my illiteracy. At the height of my success, I would sign any document or contract that people put in front of me—I would just take their word about what was on the page. Years later, my wife, Carole, would get me out from under so many terrible contracts that saw the bulk of my money going to places it shouldn't have been going. For example, for years I had been having checks sent to a promotion whose partner was dead. I was paying a dead guy my money, brudda!

"Jimmy couldn't write English, and when we went overseas I would fill out his paperwork. They asked about his destination, how long he'd be in the country, his height, weight, and sex. I would put 'Once a month, sometimes twice a week.' Immigration didn't find it funny, and they would give Jimmy dirty looks. They would ask, 'What does this mean?' And I would say, 'Oh, he didn't understand the question.'"
—Rocky Johnson, WWE Hall of Famer

To this day, I can only make out a few words. I'm not proud of it, but I just can't read or write. Not being able to learn at the same pace as other kids probably made me act out even more at home and in school. We didn't have TV or anything, and instead of going to school or doing household chores, I'd play sports with friends or go out on my own. With the other kids, I remember we would play baseball on a dirt field and pretend it was a fancy ballpark. I couldn't wait to play sports and to leave the mess at home. I got beat for it, but it was worth it. And just because I couldn't read or write didn't mean I was not smart. I figured out everything that was not on a page pretty easily by just looking at it, brudda. It was like when I started wrestling—I could just watch someone do something in the ring, and then I could match it. I observe a lot of things, brudda. I watch first and speak second. I want to make sure I truly understand something before I open my mouth.

I look back now and wish I had gone to school and learned to read and write. It hasn't been easy to go through my whole life not knowing the English language. I have always needed to depend on people to read to me. And it's not just that. Even today, some interviewers use big words and I don't understand them. Sometimes I answer the question wrong, and that is because I just don't understand what they asked me. But I still try to answer them because it's disrespectful not to. That is why I just try my best and put some words together that I think make sense.

"I made wonderful decisions athletically but poor ones academically. I had a bunch of excuses—they said it was eye problems at first, but I know I was lazy academically. Now, I've read the same book over a hundred times. I want to read 5,000 words a minute before I die. It's never too late to read, Jimmy."
—Bob Backlund, former WWF heavyweight champion

THE ISLAND WAS MY EDUCATION

The way I think of it, the islands were my education. It was all the education the Superfly needed, brudda! The islands taught me so much about life and everything. I couldn't read any books, so my education was the ocean and my surroundings. The islands bring you this certain feeling, and they make you ask "What am I doing here? This is the Heavenly Father's place!" Growing up there, it looks just like it did in the movies. I would be outside so much—whether it was fishing or playing sports—that my family had nicknamed me "Muddy" because I liked to get dirty all the time. As a matter of fact, you could have called me a fish because I never met an ocean I didn't dive right into. I would dive in and catch lobsters for my mom to eat. I was always fascinated with things outside—it didn't matter what it was. I just had to know something about everything and try it all. Forget Ric Flair—I love the brudda—but I was the real "Nature Boy."

> "Jimmy and I were kind of explorers. He'd want to take a look here or there or climb up something. In that respect, he was a good brother. He always had me going along looking at stuff I probably would never have gotten into myself. We never thought of the consequences. Then around dinner time, when the sun's getting ready to go down, we would look at each other and go, 'Uh-oh.'"
> —Henry Reiher

Back in the Gilbert Islands, I would watch all the men fish and I learned from them by watching and listening. I would go out on the boats with them, and I would catch fish and bring them home for my mom. I was on the beach with my spear almost every day looking for fish. When the bombs were dropped during World War II, they made huge holes in the reef. I figured out that when the tide went out, the fish would get left in the holes. The holes were huge—as big as a house. I would fish in five or six of these reefs. My mom would just ask me for a lobster, and I would go get her some. That is where I had my pet shark, which I called "Eat Me." He was just a baby when I found him. I fed him fish that I caught and he would follow me. I would spear the fish, and as soon as he would see the fish move, he was right on it. Later he ate right out of my mouth.

One day the tide went out, allowing me to walk all the way out to the reef. I told my mom I wanted to show her something. I tapped the water, and Eat Me knew that it was me. My mom said, "Watch out, there is a tiger shark!" I told her he was my pet. She didn't like that, so I got in the water and showed her how we swam together. I just had to be careful. He would bump into me when we swam.

When we left the Gilbert Islands, I wanted to let him go into the ocean because I knew the island people would eat him. I took a rope and tied it around his neck like a dog leash. When the tide came up, I pulled him with me to one of the passways that led into the sea. He followed me back, so I did it a few times, and then one day I never saw him again.

My stepdad would sometimes leave for months at a time on the ship, so it was just my mom and us kids. I have to be honest— I loved it when he was away. I was the man of the house and took care of my mother. I treated her the way my stepfather should have—with respect. She would just call my name and I was there. It was just my mom, Henry, and me. My mom liked to play tennis at the court that the military built for the men that had been stationed there. I remember she was a good tennis player.

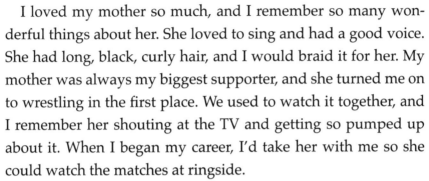

I loved my mother so much, and I remember so many won-derful things about her. She loved to sing and had a good voice. She had long, black, curly hair, and I would braid it for her. My mother was always my biggest supporter, and she turned me on to wrestling in the first place. We used to watch it together, and I remember her shouting at the TV and getting so pumped up about it. When I began my career, I'd take her with me so she could watch the matches at ringside.

My mom's favorite was Handsome Johnny Barend, and she did not like Curtis Iaukea. I would tell her that Curtis was a good friend of mine and a good brudda, and she would say, "I don't care, I don't like him." She didn't like Ripper Collins be-cause she thought he was a *maho*. I told her that when I wrestled Ripper Collins, I would put him in a headlock and he would suck on my tit. I would pound him on the head and say, "Here is your receipt, brudda." He didn't do that again, at least not to me.

I still remember her crying during my early matches because she was concerned I was getting too beat up. She'd go up to my opponents during the matches and yell, "Don't you ever hit my son!" I'd have to tell her to sit down and explain that no one was really beating me up. But that was my mother. She didn't want to see me hurt in the ring after so many years of being hurt by my stepfather. She was always my guardian angel.

> "She was the apple of his eye. He was very protective over her, like he was over all of us. Even later on when he was wrestling, when he was on business or pleasure, he'd always stay with her even though he had a hotel room. She loved wrestling, and Jimmy would take her to matches and get her autographs. She was just so proud he was able to make something of himself."
> —Louise Reiher

Everything was just lovely in the islands, brudda. The environment just mellows you out and makes you think beautiful thoughts. I still go back there for a pick-me-up today. You just stop and look at the trees, you look at the flowers, and you see all these different colors. You see the papayas and the coconuts in the trees—some are green, and some are ripe. Everything just grows wild there and there's so much to do. And all the islands I've lived on are all different, but all the same. I'm most at peace when I'm alone in nature. I continue to go back there every time I need to check my head.

A LOST CHILDHOOD

The Marshall Islands were made up of more than 30 small islands. One of them was the Bikini Atoll, and terrible things happened there. I grew up fast seeing the outcome of the famous Castle Bravo bomb testing. President Harry S. Truman had ordered testing of nuclear weapons just in case of an atomic war. I was around 12 years old, and I didn't really know what was happening. The people were brought into the coast guard station near where we lived on Ebi, and I helped the coast guard carry the people on stretchers and put them on old army beds in these big tents. They brought in hundreds of people there—I remember seeing it all, and it was shocking. They were all crying and in pain. Some were missing arms and legs. Others had burns all over their bodies. The nurses showed me how to clean up the dried blood so they could see what was wrong with the people and treat them. I also remember the doctors and nurses teaching me how to treat burns and wrap the injuries. There was so much moaning and groaning. Brudda, I still see those images today in my mind. It's in my head every day, and it has never gone away. It cannot go away. It's impossible.

You wouldn't believe the whole scene there. It was like something out of a bad movie. It was so terrible, brudda. We all knew about it on the island, but a lot of these terrible injuries weren't talked about in the news. But I saw it with my own eyes, brudda. I just wanted to help out. I didn't give it another thought—I just wanted to help those people. I was a little scared, and I didn't really understand what was happening, but it was so sad to see all the kids hurt.

It's always difficult talking about my childhood, because in many ways, I never really had a real one, brudda. Getting beaten at home was one thing, but I also saw things no one should've seen.

LEARNING WHO I REALLY WAS

When I became a teenager, I found out the real reason Bernie hit me harder than Henry or my mother. Like I said, it always seemed like I rubbed my stepfather the wrong way. I was not even 15 yet when my mother sat us down and told me that the four children she had with Bernie—Henry, Agnes, Louise, and Vicky—were my half-siblings. I remember being very, very shocked at the news, but I'd had my suspicions. I always wondered why my siblings were lighter-skinned then I was. I'm considered Polynesian, but I'm darker-skinned. I consider myself "half-cast"—black from being Fijian, and half white. Most of all, and more importantly, I wondered why I was the only one of the children who was ever beaten hard by Bernie. I loved him as much as I could, but he was probably upset with my mother for having me. Again, Bernie had his moments where he was really good to me and my mom, but the fact was I wasn't his son, and he probably punished my mom for it. He was an alcoholic, and it made him more difficult to be around. He was already a very strict man who didn't love me as much as the others because I was from another man. When he started drinking a lot, it only made him that much worse.

> "We got to where Mom and Dad were fighting a lot, and other things were going on that us kids didn't know or understand. Then one day she sat us down and told us the truth about who Jimmy was. At first, it was kind of shocking, but we all decided he was still our brother. My dad beat us so much, and he blamed Jimmy because he wasn't his own son, or that's what she thought. Maybe he regretted it—I don't know."
> —Henry Reiher

There were many times I mouthed off to Bernie, but brudda, I never really stood up to my stepfather. There were times I questioned what he was doing, but I was just a kid and didn't want to deal with it. That's why I often wanted to run away and play sports or just try to run away altogether. I used to do that a lot. Having said that, I remember there was one time I did get in the way of my father beating on my mother. Brudda, I got beat real good because of it. I was 14 or 15 when I stepped in, and he easily knocked me on my ass. My mom just cried. She couldn't do anything about it.

Bernie would sometimes apologize for what he did, but it was never enough. Getting hit made me realize I wanted no part of confrontations. I don't like dealing with heavy stuff. That's something that has stuck with me as an adult. If I have a problem with you, I will either say my piece or simply walk out of the room and do my own thing. I'd rather calm down on my own

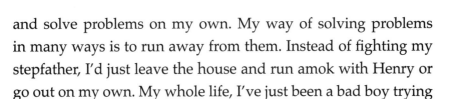

and solve problems on my own. My way of solving problems in many ways is to run away from them. Instead of fighting my stepfather, I'd just leave the house and run amok with Henry or go out on my own. My whole life, I've just been a bad boy trying to be a good man. That's the bottom line.

> "I thought he beat me and Jimmy about the same, but I think Jimmy got the harder beatings because he was older. When I was in my forties, I asked my dad why he beat me and Jimmy so much when we were little kids. My dad said that was the only thing he knew how to do."
> —Henry Reiher

I know I've written a lot here about how Bernie would beat up on us, but I do want to say again that I loved him. It's important for me to say I had some good times with my stepfather. For example, he let me on the Gilbert Islands ship when I was younger. He had been the engineer of the ship, and he let me go for fun. I was the only boy on the boat with about 10 men. These men taught me how to steer the boat and how to walk on the boat in rough waters. My stepfather took me down to the engine room to teach me how it worked. I got seasick at first, but I got over it.

I remember we used to go island to island picking up copra—the dried kernel of a coconut—for anyone who needed it. The ship would pull into port, and the islanders would load or unload the copra and fill up on ship supplies. We would stay a couple days at a time fishing and swimming. I remember I once found a dog floating in the water. Someone had thrown it away in a copra bag. I went out to get it and brought it back to land, but I had to let it go because we couldn't take dogs on the boat. It didn't seem right to leave it.

BECOMING A MAN AND COMING INTO MY OWN

In many ways, I was always my own man, even as a teenager. So, when my family decided to move to Hawaii when I was 15 or so, I didn't want to go. Bernie had gotten a job there and wanted to move us all to Wahiawa. I had already gotten used to living without them from my days in boarding school, so I told my mother I wanted to stay in the islands. My mind was set.

I had been working on a navy base in Kwajalein in the marine department. I did anything they needed. One day, I'd be driving the forklift, and another day I'd be driving boats. I liked it there, and I was playing baseball with the military and having a lovely time. After each game, I would stay overnight on the boat and then go get the islanders from Ebi and bring them to the base to work. I had it made, brudda. I had food and my own cabin. I also had plenty of time to chase after girls—or the other way around! I never had any problems in that department, brudda. I didn't need to be a superstar in a wrestling ring to get girls. They just came to me.

I think I was 15 when I had sex for the first time. My memory is not what it used to be, but I do remember it was around that time that the Superfly started making love, brudda. The Superfly never had any problem with the women. Girls loved this brudda, and I loved them so much. When I had sex for the first time, I liked it, but I don't remember who it was with. That may be hard to believe, but it's true. I don't remember her name. I don't remember much about her at all. It was a real pokey pokey, and I had a lot of those. I will say this: if I could have gotten all the girls in the island, I would have tried. I thought I was a pretty good-looking guy back then, so I was confident. I kept myself healthy, and because I messed around so much with sports, I had a good body. I was so hot back then, I remember girls would sometimes even send their brothers over to tell me they'd like to meet me. The Superfly had it all back then, brudda.

Back in the day, it was always pretty hard for me to get rid of the girls. It probably would be now too, but this brudda is a married man! When I was in the Marshall Islands, I remember swimming to different islands to look for girls. I liked to swim with sharks, brudda. I would tie up coconuts—you know the little strings they had—and float with them. I figured that out on my own, and I'd swim up to different islands and get with a girl—kiss them, hug them, whatever. I wanted them all, and they wanted me.

Like sports, wrestling, and everything the Superfly has done, sex just came naturally to me. I was a little rascal when I was young. When I liked something, I made sure I got it. The same rule applied to women, and it was lovely. The thing you need to know about me is I've never done anything half-assed in my life. Whenever I do anything, I do it with total commitment, brah. You've got to do that. You have to want something and want to be the best at something. If somebody told me I couldn't do something, I'd just do it anyway. And if something interested me, I pursued it. The Superfly was interested in many, many ladies, and I always got them, brudda.

PLAYING BALL IN HAWAII

I've already told you I dove off cliffs when I was younger. Standing on the rock is one feeling, diving off is another feeling...

then there's the feeling of being in the air and falling down. I would open my arms and just feel the air. I would wait until the last minute and then bring my hands together over my head and hit the water. Oh man, it was lovely. The other kids would just jump from small rocks, but not the Superfly. I was always different. I saw the height of the rocks and then just went for it. I would do it over and over and over.

> "Growing up, I'd hear stories from different family members about when he played rugby and baseball. They would always say he played rugby barefoot and hit people so hard that people were scared to play him. One story that was told a lot was about this Samoan player who was huge. Every time he'd play my dad, he'd get really scared. My dad was a very intense person. When we would go to the gym and work out, he would be just pouring sweat. I never saw him doing something he wasn't going to give 100 percent to."
> —Jimmy Snuka Jr., Jimmy's son and professional wrestler

I really did it all back then—whether it was baseball, rugby, or cliff diving. But as time went on, baseball started to become my favorite sport. I was really good at it, and it kept getting more and more fun for me. I played every position. I taught myself how to play and mastered the techniques right away. I didn't know it then, but playing baseball would lead me to a bigger passion in my life: bodybuilding. I had always been an active boy, but I remember being amazed by these bodybuilders at the gym. Each day I'd be at the military base—either working or getting ready for an amateur baseball game against the military's team—and my eyes would bug out seeing all these larger-than-life guys

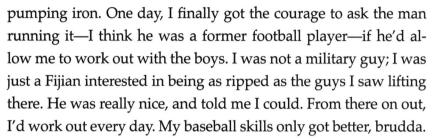

pumping iron. One day, I finally got the courage to ask the man running it—I think he was a former football player—if he'd allow me to work out with the boys. I was not a military guy; I was just a Fijian interested in being as ripped as the guys I saw lifting there. He was really nice, and told me I could. From there on out, I'd work out every day. My baseball skills only got better, brudda.

Since I was so athletic at baseball and won the team a lot of games, my new friends at the gym started raising money at the base for me to fly out to Hawaii for a tryout with the Islanders, a semipro league team. It was so nice of them to do that, but I didn't make it. They told me to go play in the Puerto Rican League and then they would give me another tryout. So, after spending a year on my own in the Marshall Islands, I left for Hawaii to try out with the team…and I made it! I had no idea what was really going on, but I tried out and was asked to sign with them right away. This was another piece of paper I signed without knowing what was on it! But I didn't care. I just wanted to play ball.

When I was on the field, people always came to watch me play. Every time I came up to bat, the outfielders would move back, but I would still hit it over their heads. I hit the ball out of the park back on to the Likiliki Highway. There was one family that always watched me play. After each game, we would go out to the bar, and eventually they thought it might be nice to set me up with their daughter. I fell in love with this woman, Carol Perry, almost instantly. She was a sweet Portuguese girl, and she was a little younger than me. We got married after dating a little while, and moved into a small apartment. There was no question I was too young to get married—and so was she. We were not ready to be in a committed relationship. One day, I found her in a car with a guy who played on a softball team. Right away, I said, "That's it...bye." I never saw her again. That was it, brah. I don't even remember a lot about her. I was young and stupid and didn't know any better. Neither did she, and that was that. I don't really count that as a marriage, even though it was. It didn't mean much to me.

I continued to play ball after breaking up with Carol. I was mainly a catcher, but I played all outfield and infield positions and I played them all really well. After playing in that summer league, I caught the eye of several major league scouts from the New York Yankees, the Philadelphia Phillies, and the Pittsburgh Pirates. They sent letters inviting me to try out for their teams, but my coach, Phillip Minicola, stood in the way. He was a bad man who was jealous of me and wouldn't release me. The dumb coach couldn't believe I got these letters because he thought he was better than me. My mom tried talking to him since I couldn't speak English well, but he refused to sign the release. He made fun of me for being from a small island. He said something like, "Did they just throw a dart at a map and find you?" My mother was so upset that I quit playing for him that day.

I know I would've gone to the major leagues if I had tried out with any of those baseball teams. I would have been something on any of those teams, brudda! Like I said, I really was a star on the field, and being that I don't half-ass anything, I know I would've become a star at baseball. But sometimes things happen for a reason. It was probably a blessing that I didn't ever play professional baseball, because I changed my focus to wrestling in the ring. Can you imagine if I had become a baseball star and never wrestled a day in my life? I can't, brudda! Where would professional wrestling be without the Superfly?

> "The other players were college graduates and all that stuff, and Jimmy could hardly speak English. He said they were throwing their dirty socks at him after practice. They were jealous. Jimmy would hit the ball out of the stadium, and with that arm of his he'd throw from the outfield all the way home. He told me he wasn't coming back—'Not the way these guys are treating me.' I said talk to the manager, but he said he was done. He made up his mind. It was like he was back at school again. He couldn't get any help."
> —*Henry Reiher*

I didn't completely quit baseball after that. It was still in my veins, brudda. I still played in the bar league and continued to kick ass on the field. My mom was always so supportive. She came to all my games and cheered me on. She would even go to the bar with me after the games to celebrate my victories or my at-bats. Bernie never saw me play, which was frustrating. My sisters did. I was having a good time.

THE HAWAIIAN LIFESTYLE

For three years I lived with my family again, and I delivered beer kegs to restaurants and bars around Honolulu for the distributor Johnston & Buscher. I had grown up around alcohol—my mom and stepfather drank a lot—but I never drank much. It was a cool thing when I worked there to drink a little with my friends, but I never abused it like I would later on in my life when I wrestled with the boys. I was just drinking to look cool, but it was not hard and heavy. I didn't want to be hungover when I worked out, so I'd only have one or two beers.

"It was hard for us because everybody knew Jimmy,
and because he worked for a Beefeater [distributor],
we couldn't sneak out. We couldn't drink alcohol because
someone who knew Jimmy would be there, and we knew
they'd tell Jimmy. It was just awful. He was so protective of us."
—*Louise Reiher*

Unlike the Marshall Islands—where I'd sometimes tie ropes on the ends of branches and attach rocks to them to lift—the gym where I worked out in Hawaii had it all. I may have worked out in the islands, but I figured out how to really build my body in Hawaii. I owe that to my brother. He had a membership at this gym and gave it to me when he left for the navy. I loved to work out, and the gym's owner did, too. This man, Rex Ravell, just so happened to have played Tarzan at one time, so you know I loved and idolized him right away. He was larger than life, brah. He just had this look about him. He was everything to me, brudda. He was my idol—a real-life Tarzan! I wanted to look just like him, and he taught me so much. He was a very nice, relaxed guy.

Everybody in Hawaii is so nice and calm. They treat everybody kindly, and I try to live that way to this day. It's not like how it is in New York City or some other big cities. Don't get me wrong—I love everybody. Life is too short to hate people, brudda. Hawaii is a true love of mine, just like the Fiji, Gilbert, and Marshall islands before it. I still go back to this day—it is everything I am. Every time I've been in the ring, I show people where I came from by using the hand gesture I always do. You know what it is, brudda! It's the ILY sign, and I've used it throughout my career. I started using it in Portland because I didn't speak English well. I saw the hand sign in a comic book and thought I would use it. It's my way of saying I love you, brudda!

"It's amazing how Hawaii never left him. There are so few of us out there who grew up in Hawaii and have made it big. This is a guy who grew up in Hawaiian culture, and made himself successful. Listening to him now, he still has that pidgin talk. It took me back home. Here is a guy who never forgot where he came from. I looked up to Jimmy as a kid. Growing up in Hawaii, I was definitely a fan of the WWE and wrestling. I used to jump off my bed, think I was Snuka, and land on pillows."
—Shane Victorino, *Major League Baseball player*

CHAPTER 2
BODY OF WORK

"Coming home from school, he was always at home waiting around. One day, I said, 'What's your plan?' He told me he honestly didn't know. He and I used to watch Tarzan movies, and the closest thing at home was professional wrestling. I threw that at him, and told him he could become a wrestler. Little did I know how much that was going to play out thereafter."

—Henry Reiher

Eventually Rex's gym closed, so I moved to another place called the Power in Waikiki. The new gym would really set me on my life path, brudda. It was owned by professional wrestler Dean Higuchi, who was better known as Dean Ho. His gym was home for all the bodybuilders in town and for professional wrestlers whenever they had matches in the area on the weekends. It was cool to work out at Ho's place. I remember being with my mother and watching him in the ring. It was crazy for a kid like me to hang out with him and to become friends with the other wrestlers. He also taught me martial arts. Thankfully I never really needed to use it. The Superfly is more of a lover than a fighter!

Performers like King Curtis and Sammy Steamboat became fast friends of mine, and so did many others. I think they took to me because I looked jacked. I had this muscular body from playing baseball and running around all those years, and I worked out for hours every day. The more I pumped, the more I became close friends, even brothers, with these guys. With their advice, I started seriously getting into bodybuilding. I began taking steroids, which were totally legal at the time, and I had muscles popping out all over my body. I didn't really know what steroids were. I took powders and pills, and never injected myself with anything. I just thught they were vitamins or something. As always, I wanted to be the best, and I still felt the desire to be Tarzan.

I entered into a few bodybuilding contests and won them. One of them was the Mr. Hawaiian Island competition. I didn't win any money or anything, just a trophy, but I was proud of myself. I worked my ass off to get that trophy. Before I went on stage, I remember thinking, *I'm ready, and I want to win. If I get up there, I don't want to lose or come in second.* I felt I was in better shape than the rest of the guys. I had to diet so the judges could see how ripped I was. I was starving myself, brudda! I wanted to do other things with my life, and I knew this would help me.

While I was training for that competition, I started to wrestle with some of my friends. They taught me how to do some moves, and I taught them how to build their bodies. By the time I won Mr. Hawaiian Island, my friends and I were convinced there was real money for me in wrestling, so I focused on that full time.

One guy who saw me kicking ass in the weight room changed my life forever, brudda. His name was Cowboy Frankie Laine, and he was an old-school wrestler from Toronto. Laine was in Hawaii to wrestle a bunch of shows and to see his girlfriend. He

asked me to help him work out in exchange for some wrestling training, and I couldn't resist. Laine was the first guy who really brought me into the wrestling world. He taught me everything. I did not know anything about professional wrestling. I wrestled in the sand at school when I was a kid, but he taught me the names of the holds and when to use them. Each day, he'd take me to the gym and teach me the routines. He'd show me how to lock up, how to do different holds, and how to take bumps.

It all came easy to me, brudda. Originally, Frankie was supposed to be in Hawaii for three months before heading back to his own promotion. But he convinced his promoter to let him stay on the island. He was such a good guy, and he saw so much talent in me. Without Frankie, who knows where I would've ended up? Thanks to him, I ended up going to Portland, Oregon, to wrestle. Laine knew the promoter there, Don Owens, and he talked me up to him.

CREATING THE SUPERFLY SPLASH

I knew right away what I wanted my finisher to be when I decided to be a wrestler. I had no fear when I dove off those cliffs back in the day, and I wanted that to be evident in the ring, too. Just like I loved flying into the water after diving off the cliffs, I told Frankie I wanted to soar off the top rope. He didn't hesitate for a minute. I remember saying to him, "Brudda, you have been in this business for a long time—do you mind if I practice diving off the top rope on you?" He agreed without giving it much thought. We were very close, and I jumped onto him one time and that was it. I'd perfected it the more I kept doing it, but I knew what I wanted to do and how it could be done without hurting anybody.

> "Jimmy 'Superfly' Snuka set the standard for the splash from the top rope. Fans always want to compare my 5-Star Frog Splash with Jimmy's legendary finishing move. We've all seen him defeat many notable superstars with this spectacular move, but I think I'm most impressed that he was jumping off that top rope with bare feet!"
> —Rob Van Dam, Impact Wrestling and former WWE and ECW star

I remember telling Frankie one day the same thing I've told all of my opponents ever since: never close your eyes when I'm giving you the Superfly splash. Just make sure you listen to me, and we'll be okay. You have to have trust when you're in the ring with someone. I explained to him that while he was lying down, he needed to sit up halfway and put his hands on his sides as I landed on him. While I was in midair, I slowly started cupping my body and used my knees to break my fall. That way, we ended up breaking the fall together. The goal is to create as little impact as possible, but for it to look like I'm destroying him. Nobody gets hurt when this is done right. That's what makes the splash such a great move. It looks like it's incredibly painful, but when it's done right and received right, the opponent feels nothing, brudda.

> "As a high-flyer, I loved Jimmy Snuka. I got to take the Superfly splash once when I was on the indie circuit in the mid-to-late 1990s, and I was so stoked to be taking it. Then he hit me with it, and my pancreas shot out of my ass! It was safe, but it was stiff. Afterward, I was still a fan—I just never wanted to get hit with the Snuka splash again!"
> —Shane Helms, aka "The Hurricane"

Thankfully, no one has really gotten hurt from being on the receiving end of my splash. The Superfly, however, has gotten hurt plenty of times, brudda. I come down like a parachute, and if you meet me halfway, it all goes well. I always make sure the other guy doesn't get hurt. But about 15 or 20 years ago, I had two guys in different matches who didn't listen. I tore both of my triceps from people catching me wrong. Two guys—I don't remember who—just forgot what to do. They screwed up and lay there flat with their hands out. I had to turn in midair and got screwed up.

Many years later, I was wrestling Metal Maniac, who was my brudda and loved to eat. We went out and ate some steaks before the match, and he ate his so fast it was like he chewed it and swallowed it in one gulp. When we got to the arena, I asked him if he was okay. He knew I was going to splash him, and at that point, we'd probably had a hundred matches before and he'd taken the splash many times.

So, I brought him to the center of the ring, I climbed up to the top rope, and I came down on him real good. Next thing I knew, I smelled something. Oh man, the ref called, "1...2...3" and I was like, "Let's get the hell out of here." After the match, we went back to the locker room, and his pants had nothing but shit inside, brudda! I warned him he ate too much too fast!

> "What he did was so incredibly innovative. Nobody ever dared to go off the top rope. That's like going to the top of a 20-foot cage today. Jimmy Snuka really opened the door to a lot of different, awesome ideas for wrestlers. If he didn't do that, wresting would still be inside the ring and on the tarp only. He is the first and he is without question the best high flyer we've ever seen."
> —Kurt Angle, Impact Wrestling and former WWE star and Olympic gold-medalist

THE BIRTH OF JIMMY "SUPERFLY" SNUKA

My wrestling name was changed a couple of times, but that never mattered to me. It didn't matter what the promoters called me as long as I had fun and got paid. But over time, I started thinking James Smith didn't fit who I was. I wanted people to call me Tarzan, but knew it'd be too unoriginal. I wrestled a few matches in Hawaii as Jimmy Kealoha, the last name meaning "the loved one." I also used the name Big Snuka in the years to come, but Jimmy Snuka eventually just stuck.

I had wanted Snuka in my name, because it reminded me of my roots. Back in the Fiji Islands, snooker tables are very popular, and all the cool guys who played it and hung around the bars were called "snukas." I wanted to pay tribute to where I came from, but also have a new identity. The "Superfly" part of my name would come later. It was an easy piece to add—I used to be called that after diving from the cliffs back in the day.

In a lot of ways, I had the character Jimmy "Superfly" Snuka in my head since I was a kid. When I was young, I would look at the birds when they'd take off and wonder, *Could I do that?* I took that approach with everything. When I saw weightlifters, I thought, *Could I do that?* When I saw baseball being played, I thought, *Could I do that?* Deep down, I knew I could.

It was around the time I competed in that bodybuilding contest that I met Sharon Liana Ili in Laie, Hawaii. I was playing rugby at the time and my team was playing her school, the Church College of Hawaii, in a tournament. Over the course of a couple months, I became friends with her and her three sisters, who had been watching the games. After the games, we would all hang out, and one time Sharon asked us to come see her dance at the nearby Polynesian Cultural Center. I remember thinking, *I wonder what this is all about?* and *Maybe I'll give it a break.* What I mean by that is there were four sisters and they were all pretty, so I figured I'd get with one of them. As the rugby season went on, we would spend a lot of time together as a group without anything happening. But after our team won the tournament and the season ended, I started dating Sharon. She was a nice, pretty girl, and we got along very well.

Sharon's parents were very protective of her—they wouldn't let us go out alone without a chaperone. I remember Henry dated one of Sharon's sisters so that I could date Sharon. Henry eventually stopped going out with her because he thought they were grooming him for one of the other sisters, and he didn't want that. I played rugby in Laie and we would have barbecues at Sharon's house. At the time I was still working for Johnston & Buscher and still training at the gym, plus playing baseball. After a while, Sharon's parents got to like me and allowed me to sleep on their sofa. I even helped build an addition to the family home for Sharon and me.

After about three months of dating, Sharon told me she was pregnant. I was happy, but I didn't want to be tied down. It was 1969—I was in the best shape of my life and had plans to wrestle professionally. Frankie Laine and I already had plans to go to Portland. Sharon and her family were nice people, so I did the right thing. A justice of the peace married us before I left for Portland. I told her I'd send for her eventually, and I meant it. I didn't want my child to grow up in the same situation I had, not having his real father around. On the other hand, my mother did not like Sharon. Sharon was Samoan, and the older Fijian did not like Samoans. Aside from that, I know we got married for the wrong reason. We had many good moments together, but we never really connected.

Frankie and I left for Portland from Kaimuki, Hawaii, when I was about 25 years old, and my mom and Sharon eventually followed me. My mother moved in with us. After that, my brother and sisters moved to the mainland, too. I took care of them, and

I even took care of Sharon's family later on in life. I built an addition to our home with the help of Sharon's dad, who was a carpenter. I paid for the lumber and supplies, and together we built a home. When Sharon's mom and dad moved back to Western Samoa, Sharon's sister took over the family land in Hawaii.

Sharon's dad was some kind of chief in Western Samoa, and he gave me the name Chief Paku. It was a title passed down to chiefs of land. Specifically, I was I'aulualo, which is the chief name, of the village of Palauli. It's a big deal, brah. There is a ceremony with kava and other High Chiefs. It's tradition in the Samoan culture. I hope to pass it onto my son.

> **"That name is a very big deal...it's partly because of the history of the name. It's such a high title to be given by someone. You must accept the name, and I have not done so. I appreciate the title, but I also know it's not to be taken lightly."**
> —*Jimmy Snuka Jr.*

My mom had separated from Bernie by the time she came to Portland. She had been working for several years as a live-in nanny, leaving Bernie alone with three kids, which he didn't like. They eventually split up and he got remarried. Once I left for Portland, I never saw Bernie again. Years later he'd come to visit in the mainland, but I was wrestling in Japan. Bernie ended up dying of natural causes, I think, in 2003. My mom eventually remarried a nice man, Russell McClean, in Portland.

I'm sure Sharon wished I hadn't left for Portland, but she and my mom knew nothing they could say could keep me in Hawaii. I was going to wrestle and become a superstar. It was very hard to leave them at first. I didn't think I would be gone so long. I thought I would be able to visit often. But I was so busy, I never saw my family regularly again after that.

"TCB" AND THE KING: MEETING ANOTHER IDOL

You may not know it, but a lot of my inspiration in life comes from Elvis Presley. Tarzan was my idol in the Fiji Islands, but once I was in Hawaii, I fell in love with The King. Ever since I hit it big in TV wonderland, I've signed my autographs with a "TCB." Elvis had signed his the same way. That's what both of us have done from day one—we take care of business, brudda. Elvis was a real man, and I just loved his voice, his robes—I loved it all. I used to listen to him all the time, and when I was in Hawaii in 1973, I got to see him up close. First, I had seen him coming off the helicopter, and let me tell you, that scene was crazy, brudda.

There were tons of screaming people there trying to see him and holding up signs. I was lucky to spot him. He was just too cool. Then, I was working security for the Polynesian Cultural Center, where he was visiting while in town for a concert at the Blaisdell Center in Honolulu, and I saw him even closer. I was supposed to be crowd control, keeping the people away from him, but I was star struck. I wish I had been able to go to his concert, but tickets were sold out in a flash.

Years later I was wrestling in Memphis, and I had heard from someone that Elvis was in the building. Someone told me he had been watching the matches from a private spot, but I don't know if that was true. If I had known, I would've run up to him and shook the brudda's hand!

LIFE IN PORTLAND AND TRAVELING AROUND

I may be older now, and my memory may not be what it once was—those flying head butts didn't help—but I still remember how natural it felt moving around the ring like Tarzan when I debuted in Portland. I fell in love with wrestling in the Pacific Northwest. Don Owens was a good promoter, and I really liked him. He was a little guy, skinny with dark and thinning hair. He was a redneck-cowboy type who rode horses on his farm. I remember that farm, brudda. Horses, cows...you name it. Don was a very good promoter, and his events were almost always sold out. The pay was good at the time, too, and the money was always there when he said it would be. He was an honest man. He was not like some of the cockroaches you find in the business. He and I hit it off right away.

I remember that after seeing my moves and how I carried myself in the ring, Don told Frankie, "You did really good with this kid. He's going to make us some money." You've got to under-stand that I was a different kind of man back then. I was a body-builder. I looked like I could get anything I wanted. I had worked so hard for it, so when I got in the ring, the adrenaline just kicked in. Each night, seven days a week, I'd do an independent show. I was stunned to get paid $15 per match. It was not a ton of money, but I was just in love with wrestling. There is a high, a medium, and a low to everything, brah, and wrestling was the highest high for me when I started out. I loved it, brudda—so much so I remember thinking, *I get paid for this? Cool!*

When I think about it now, my first bumps weren't in the ring—they were messing around with nature. Spending time running around the jungle, there were plenty of times I got hurt, but I just picked myself up and went right back at it. The islands taught me that lesson. With that mind-set, I tried everything without giving it too much thought. I'd surf on rocky waters or walk over hot coals. It didn't matter to me. I just wanted to try stuff out. It was the same way in the ring, brudda.

> "Jimmy didn't perform for the money. I saw a couple guys like that—The Dynamite Kid was another one. They not only performed for the crowd, they also performed for their peers. Nothing made Jimmy happier than hearing one of the boys say, 'By God, Jimmy, that was a great match.' You'd see a smile so wide on his face. He wanted his peers to recognize him as the best, and he *was* one of the very best. He had this inward desire. That's why he had such great matches. It was a competition out there, and he went out every night knowing he was going to steal the show."
> —*Terry Funk, wrestling icon and WWE Hall of Famer*

Wrestling came easy for me, but I'm not going to lie—it took me quite some time to get used to Portland. I was used to the trees and the beauty of the islands, not the industrial life of a big city. And don't get me started on the weather, brudda. Being cold was tough for me to digest. The snow and the cold freaked me out. Frankie had told me to buy some new clothes, but I couldn't believe how cold it was. I missed the warm weather and island life. I also missed walking around barefoot. Most of the time, when I wasn't wrestling, I kept busy by weightlifting inside. It was too damn cold outside to do anything else! When I went to Portland, I did an exhibition for Sam Loprinzi at his gym. I only did the exhibition for the Mr. Oregon contest. It worked because I was advertising the wrestling events that way.

"You had to be 13 years old to get a membership at Loprinzi's gym, so I lied to get in. I rode my bike there to just sit and watch Jimmy work out. Every exercise he did, I tried to emulate. The thing I remember most is at the end of a workout, he'd slowly do these concentrated curls. The dumbbells were lightweight, 20 or 25 pounds, and he'd just sit there and just go slow with this twisting motion. He would sit there for 20 minutes. I remember asking him, 'Mr. Snuka, how can I get as big as you?' He looked at me and smiled, and he just said, 'Kid, just keep coming and working out.' He made it sound so simple. He'd watch me, and just shake his head in approval and say, 'That's it, kid,' or rub the top of my head. There was a tender side to him. To this day, I still do the exercises that he showed me when I was not even 13. At one time, I had 21-inch arms, and I attribute that to him. Guys used to ask me how I got those arms, and if I liked the guy, I'd show him and tell him where it came from. I owed Jimmy that much."

—Matt Borne, the original Doink the Clown

It was not just the weather I had to get used to in Portland. Just like when I was growing up, I quickly had to learn a new dialect. They spoke so differently in Portland then they did in Hawaii or the islands. They also looked different. All the women had makeup and weird hairdos. In the Marshall Islands and Hawaii, a lot of people looked the same. In Portland, it was a cultural shock. It was like taking all the colors in the world and mixing them up.

I wrestled in Portland every night, seven days a week, on and off for almost eight years. I just kept getting better and better. I figured out that I had to take my time in the ring. All of the guys felt that way, brah. It wasn't like it is now, where everything is a rush. I was taught to take everything slow, and to build stories in the ring at a slower pace. That style is missed today.

Wrestling back in the 1970s and 1980s was so very different than it is today. I'm sure you've read many articles, seen a lot of footage on YouTube, read many other wrestlers' autobiographies, and know all about what wrestling was like back then. It's hard to imagine now, because Vince McMahon just rules the wrestling world, but there were territories throughout the country where wrestling was the biggest thing and everyone had a piece of the pie. I wrestled for the National Wrestling Alliance (NWA), which included Portland, Texas, San Francisco, Georgia, and Florida. I bounced around those territories, but mostly wrestled in Portland.

"I was at one of his first matches in Portland, if not his first. I had heard my dad talking to the others about what a phenomenal athlete he was, and that he was the best talent he'd ever seen in the business. My father loved him. He had so much respect for him as an athlete. They just clicked, and Jimmy took a liking to me right away. Being Tony Borne's son, I was able to be in a confined area where wrestlers walked by me to enter the ring. I remember Jimmy walking by for the first time, and I was in total awe at his presence. He was just unbelievable—his energy, the look in his eye, his physique. He was the total package.

"When he'd start to make his comeback, he'd stand there and just flex. He'd then start this Polynesian dance. He would want to rush it, but the guys he was in there with, like Playboy Buddy Rose, would tell him, 'Dance…just dance.' The crowd would be going nuts to see him kick ass, but it was better to make them wait for it. He was learning how to get the most of everything. Even when he wrestled for the WWF, he would take his time.

"That's not done anymore. Before Jimmy climbed up the cage, he would look up there first. He'd be standing there on the floor, and he'd just look at the top. People knew what he was thinking, but he wouldn't start climbing the cage. He would look up there, then look down, look around, and then look up again. Then, he'd very slowly climb up there. And when he perched himself up and jumped off, it was absolutely phenomenal."
—Matt Borne

I loved wrestling every day, and the fans in Portland made me feel like I was the biggest star in the world. I worked very hard for them, and they appreciated it. I'd leave for a while and wrestle somewhere else, and then come back for a while. The way it worked back then was that if another NWA territory wanted to use a wrestler, they could. For example, if one promoter wanted to take you off his show because you just finished a storyline or you weren't as fresh, he'd offer you to another territory so you'd be fresh over there. In exchange, they'd get a kickback or take on another talent, so it worked out for everyone. For me, it was a great way to recharge my batteries. I could be away for weeks or sometimes months at a time. I always changed from heel to face when coming to a new territory. I just wanted to mix it up. And to be honest, I moved around for the money. I was not a dummy. If someone wanted to pay me more, I'd go. It was simple as that.

> **"Jimmy may not be able to read, but he can count.**
> **He can count money."**
> —Jeff Miller

Portland was my home base, where I had a home and lived with my mother and wife (and later my children). My mother loved it—she just loved watching me wrestle, brudda. She was my biggest fan, and I took her everywhere I went. When I moved to Vancouver, she lived with us. When we moved to the Carolinas, she and her new husband, Russell, lived with us.

She would always go to my wrestling events, and she would come right up to the apron. My partner would throw me out of the ring so I could take her back to her seat and make sure that she didn't get hurt. She was loud—just like she was when we'd watch wrestling together on TV. I could hear her above everyone else.

Being in Portland and wrestling in other NWA territories was great, but I didn't only stick with NWA territories. I wrestled a bit for Verne Gagne's AWA in Minneapolis–St. Paul, and made trips to Japan, which paid me a lot of money. Sharon actually gave birth to my son, James Wiley Smith Thomas Reiher Snuka—aka Jimmy Jr.—in 1971 during my first trip to Japan. I remember being so excited, even though I was not there to see him born. Everything changed for us when Jimmy Jr. arrived. I finally felt connected to the marriage. Even though Sharon and I had been married, it didn't feel real until I saw my son in person. I was just so happy to have a boy.

"When I was young, I didn't really know what was going on. I knew he was a big deal, but I didn't follow wrestling. I'd been to shows before, but I didn't realize what was going on until I was in junior high and my girlfriend at the time made me a scrapbook of my dad. It had stuff from all these different magazines and stuff I'd never seen before. I started to realize just how big he was."
—*Jimmy Snuka Jr.*

The more established I got in the business, the harder it was to turn down the ladies. I was a stud in the Marshalls and Hawaii, and that train just kept going into Portland and everywhere I traveled on the road. Having sex—"pokey pokey," as I call it—was just as common as drinking was back in the day. It didn't matter if you were married or not—girls were everywhere and were waiting for us after all our matches. I was never faithful to my wife. There were just too many women on the road, brudda. It didn't mean I didn't love my wife, it just meant I loved being with other women, too. We would go to the bar to get some drinks, a lady would walk by, and then 30 minutes later she'd leave with someone. It was just awesome. It would go on and on. Rowdy Roddy Piper once slept with a girl who he thought was my girlfriend. He told me he was nervous that I'd beat his ass for sleeping with her. It might have even been in the same day, brah! But I didn't care. It was a free-for-all in those days.

If I'm really being honest, I lost count of the number of women I slept with. I don't know if it's 2,000 or 4,000 or 10,000. I really didn't count. Sometimes, I'd have two or three in a night, brudda. There was so much hanky panky going on. Sometimes it got out of hand. You'd show up to town, and there would be two girls fighting over you, saying, "He's mine tonight!"

I was young and having a good time. I was in the right sport at the right time. Everything just came through for me. I've slept with some female wrestlers, too. The Fabulous Moolah had a wrestling school, and I had fun with some of her girls. I'm very bad with names, though, so I can't tell you who they were. And in case you're wondering, I could go all night long and protected myself all the time. I was always clean. Those were the days, brudda. You just couldn't stop it. I'm sorry to say the cheating didn't stop after Jimmy Jr. was born, either.

I was wrestling in Japan three years later when I received some terrible news. My sister Agnes, who was with the coast guard, hung herself in Ala Moana Park in 1974. No one knows for sure what happened, but she had wanted to see Bernie, and my mom, I had heard, forbid it when he was in town. My mother and sister had a fight, and later that night, it seemed she decided to end her life. I loved my sister, and the news was just so terrible when I had heard it. When I came back from Japan, I wanted to know why an investigation was not being done, but it seemed to be a clear-cut case. Agnes was an incredible woman. She was only 26 years old when she died, and had already accomplished so much in her life. She was a sergeant in the coast guard and did very well for herself, receiving honorary medals and things like that. I miss Agnes. In many ways, she was like a second mother to me. She'd take care of Henry and I whenever my mother wasn't home. She was very loving and a really down-to-earth sister. Like me, she was also very fearless—maybe even more so. I try to keep moving in my life anytime something bad like that happens. It's very easy to let time slowly pass you by, but I miss her every day.

VERNE GAGNE AND THE KIDS

Verne Gagne had asked me to check out the students at his wrestling school in St. Paul. Not too many promoters let you do your own thing, but Verne knew how good I was and probably wanted his students to learn from me. As long as they paid me right, I worked hard for any promoter. It was that simple: I go

My siblings Vicky, Henry, Agnes, and Louise

in the ring, I do my job, they pay me, and everything is okay. A lot of good wrestlers came out of Gagne's school. The Iron Sheik was there, and so were Richard Blood, aka Ricky "The Dragon" Steamboat, Ken Patera, The Killer Bees, and Ric Flair. They were all young, and were real up-and-comers. I didn't know back then that they'd become stars, but they seemed to follow me in the territories after that.

I worked a lot of matches with some of those guys, but my stay in Minnesota was short. During a match, I used my hands to break my fall after being tossed out the ring. My hand hit the bottom of an iron chair, and I landed weird and snapped my wrist. That was the end of that.

> "I met him in 1972 in Minnesota. He was just the most phenomenal athlete I'd ever seen. He broke his wrist in the first month I met him, and I remember him rubbing palm leaves on it. I was like, 'Jimmy, see a doctor.' But the island guys have their way of doing things."
> —Ric Flair, wrestling icon and WWE Hall of Famer

When I broke my left wrist, I left St. Paul. I was angry that I wasn't going to be able to work in the ring. The doctor told me it was broken and that it would never be the same again. I didn't want to hear anything like that, so I went to Hawaii to see Sharon's dad, who some people might call a witch doctor. He gave me some deep massages for about a month and I was back to work shortly thereafter. Years later, I taught my kids how to give that kind of massage, and when I'd return from the road, I had them ease my pain.

I was lucky—during my whole career that was the only major injury I ever had during a match. If I got hurt, I just taped it up, brudda. It's not like today, where you're guaranteed work and you get paid no matter what. Back in the day, you just sucked it up and went to work. That's not to say the Superfly hasn't felt pain. I've felt a world of pain, brah. But what I do to get by is go back to the island. Any medicine I need is from the islands. I'd chew on a leaf and put it on a cut, and that made me feel good. I would cook a lemon leaf and drink it for relief. We would also pound the kava roots to a powder, mix it with water, and drink it, and that'd make you feel relaxed. At the very least, it'd make you fall asleep. I don't like taking pills for pain. When I had more serious surgeries later in life, I took pills, but I have always relied on island methods, and, of course, my pot, which we call *pakalolo*. It relaxes me so much. There's a reason it's used to help cancer patients, brudda!

Once I recovered, I went back to Portland. In many territories, promoters sort of owned the wrestlers, but I never felt that way with Don. I always understood the business, and it was smooth sailing all around. I should explain that sometimes when fans read that a wrestler had problems with a promoter, it might not be true. Storylines were always built up each time one of us left town, so many fans believed it for real. Wrestling *was* real to fans back then. We had separate locker rooms for the heels and faces to keep the stories going. I never had any problems with any promoters. I made them money, and they made me money. It was that simple. I also never had problems with any other wrestlers. I loved them all, brudda.

> "We didn't hang out a whole lot. Back then, kayfabe was pretty strong, and he was working as a heel. Most of the time, there were separate locker rooms. But he was always a gentleman to work with. He treated everybody with dignity. If a guy didn't have a place to stay, he'd be invited to Jimmy's place to have a seven-course Polynesian dinner. That was Snuka."
> —Ricky "The Dragon" Steamboat, WWE Hall of Famer

Also, I called the shots, brudda. I always have. I just talk to my opponent for a few minutes before the match. That's my preparation. We're given a certain time limit, and we go over a few high spots first, and then I tell them where we take the match. That's it. That's just the way it goes. I just say, "Brudda, this is what we're going to do at the end," and we discuss the in-between a little. I am a ring general. I'm not going to change. One time I was wrestling some rookie, and he came up to me and said, "I'd like to do this with you," and he explained what he wanted to do in the ring. I just looked at him. I let him talk, then I said, "You know what, brudda. You see that broom over there? That's what you're going to wrestle tonight." He got what I meant. I was having some fun. He was probably scared of me, but I was just having some fun.

> "Anyone can teach you how to hit the ropes, but 99 percent of the time, this business is about getting in all your moves, listening to the crowd, and knowing what to do and when to do it. Jimmy's a ring general. He's the captain of the ship."
> —Jeff Miller

It was in Portland where I shared the ring with other stars and good bruddas like Andre the Giant, Buddy Rose, and Jesse Ventura. Ventura was a good worker and a good man. We didn't have much in common, though. He didn't drink with the boys and went home after the matches. He was also a heel, and back then, heels and faces couldn't hang out together.

Andre was a good guy. He was such a lovely man and had a big heart. I just loved Andre like a brother—a real brother. In the ring, he was unbelievable. He was so patient. He just let you do your own thing, and then when you tagged him, you knew the Giant was in the ring. He owned it, brah. I've heard many people had problems with Andre. I've heard that he was not nice to some people, but if you worked your ass off the same way he did, he loved you. If you didn't, he wouldn't let you get by him, brudda. Many times, I saw him grab guys by the ears or their noses and escort them out of the building if they didn't work hard enough. It was never like that between the two of us.

Whenever he was wrestling on the West Coast, he'd stay with me, and the kids just loved it. The kids couldn't get enough of him. He would pick them up and play with them. He really was a gentle giant. You hear people say that a lot about big men with big hearts, but with Andre, they meant it. This brudda was such a good man, and let me tell you, he had a big appetite. Andre could eat. I remember when we would barbecue at my house, he would eat two huge steaks and 50 chicken legs. Yes, I said chicken *legs*! He never ate the wings—he wanted the sweet meet. And Andre could drink like no other man I have ever seen. He could finish a case of beer and a few bottles of wine in one sitting. The beer can, I remember to this day, looked so damn small in his hands.

Andre and I drank a ton together. We would have the Polynesian dance group that Sharon was a member of come and dance for Andre. He loved it. Andre was quite the ladies' man. I would set him up with girls whenever he was in town. He was a big man and could handle it, brah. The girls were always curious about Andre's deal, and they wanted to be with him. Everybody was so curious about the big man. When we traveled together, we would get so many people looking at us and asking us questions. Andre was larger than life. I remember he and I went to see *Jaws* back in the day. He loved it, but the funny thing was that when that shark jumped out of the water, Andre would jump out of his seat. I laughed so hard that such a big man was afraid of a shark in a movie.

When Andre was done with a show, he always wanted to go eat, drink, and be left alone, but that never happened. We would always hang out, and we loved each other's company when we traveled to different shows together. Andre had a van he traveled in, and he would always do the driving. When he traveled by air, he had to fly first class, and it was still difficult for him to fit in his body in those little seats. I would sit next to him and just laugh watching him.

I remember one time Andre and I were going from Portland to California to wrestle, and he told me to stop at a gas station. He got out of the van and walked into the station shop. He came back with two cases of beer, and told me and his manager, Frank Valois, "Okay, now we can go to California." Andre could drink, brudda. We all could. Unfortunately, many times we were behind the wheel. Drinking and driving was normal back then—so were fender benders, I'm sure. Most of us would all drink a lot of booze after matches, and we sometimes even drank before matches, though never enough to impair us in the ring. I never

drank significantly before a match for the same reason I didn't do hard drugs before matches—we all had each other's backs because we were all in the same boat. We didn't want to hurt each other.

"Back in those days, guys went out after matches and promoters didn't care—just as long as you worked sober or were drunk but could work. It's not like it is today. I had seen Jimmy on the days he was drunk, and whatever drunk feeling he had was gone when he got in that ring. Then, I'd come to the back of his dressing room, and he'd say, 'When are we going out?' It was just part of your life back then—a routine."

—Bill Apter, wrestling journalist

I visited Andre's home many times, which was on a big ranch in Charlotte, North Carolina. As you might imagine, it was huge! His rooms were enormous, and I remember the doors were over-sized so that he'd have enough room to get through them. His bed must have been custom-made, because, brudda, they don't make beds that size. I think his bed must have been twice the size of mine. The chairs in his place were also double-sized—like chairs fit for a giant king. I think he had a daughter somewhere in there, but I'm not sure.

Andre wasn't the only guy I drank with, of course. I was a party boy. I loved going out, drinking beer, and having fun. To this day, pakalolo is still my best medicine—but I never did any of the hard stuff back then. I loved the camaraderie amongst the boys, being in the ring, and entertaining the fans, so I never wanted to risk a performance.

ME AND MY MATCHES

I tried not to get into a lot of fights with other wrestlers or fans during my career, though I easily could have. Some guys were rougher than others, and some fans were just looking for problems. Usually I just preferred to say my piece and walk away, or else pay some guys back in the ring—especially if they screwed something up. I was a good worker, and when some other guys weren't, I let them know it. We are all in this business to make money and support our families. We're in the ring because we love it, and you have to know how to work with your opponent. We're not there to demolish each other, so whenever someone hit me hard, I'd come back at them and hit them harder. I know many people were nervous about getting in the ring with me, but I just wanted things done the right way. So, if they hit me hard, I'd tell them they've got a receipt coming. I owed them one, and I never told them when I'd use it. When they least expected it, the Superfly struck.

> "Jimmy was as smooth as smooth could be and as quick as humanly possible. My brother and I prided ourselves on being very quick and very agile athletes, but Jimmy's timing was just impeccable. He was as good as anybody I've ever been in the ring with."
> —Gerald Brisco, WWE Hall of Famer and co-owner of Georgia Championship Wrestling

While I always tried to keep my fighting limited to the ring, I do remember many years later being at a bar in Georgia with Terry Gordy and the boys, and someone pushed their way in front of me. I said, "Excuse me," and this guy said, "I think I can take you down." I told the guy, "Let's just have a drink." But the guy wanted a fight. Gordy was behind him giving me hand signals, so when the guy made his move, Gordy clobbered him. All the bouncers came and took the guy outside. That was it.

Another time, I was at a bar with Road Warrior Hawk, and a fan egged him on until finally Hawk broke the guy's arm. I didn't get involved with that stuff. I saw it all around me though, brudda. Fans often like to pick fights with wrestlers.

"He was a good wrestler who didn't take any shit from anybody. He worked out very hard, and always looked good. But his heart is bigger than his whole body. I was with Jimmy on a couple of tours in Japan. I remember one time, I lost my kneepad and I had to get ready for a match. He was like, 'Here, brother,' and gave me his."
—Nikolai Volkoff, WWE Hall of Famer

FAREWELL TO PORTLAND

I kept working in Portland until the late 1970s—I just loved it. I did very well there, winning the heavyweight championship six times. The first time I remember having a belt was when I won the NWA Pacific Northwest heavyweight title against Bull Ramos on November 16, 1973. I liked working with Bull. He was a big Apache Indian, and a great guy to work with. He was a good teacher, and we taught each other in the ring. I remember he once took me to an Indian reservation. We smoked the peace pipe together, and his people gave me the name Eagle Pipe. This name was given to me because I flew like an eagle, brudda!

We all learned from each other back in the day. I teamed and held a title with another good guy, Dutch Savage. We traveled a lot together, and he had family barbecues with my family to probably get closer to me. He might've been a little jealous of the hype I was getting, but he was okay. That's how it was. Everyone had to do his own thing.

As much of a good time as I was having there, eventually I felt like it was time to leave Portland for good. I had headlined shows for so long there and won all the belts, so I sort of felt like there was nowhere else to go, brudda. Besides, other promoters were always calling for the Superfly. So, in 1977, I left the territory and headed to Dallas to wrestle for Fritz Von Erich. I kind of lost track of Frankie Laine when I left Portland. I think he went back to Canada, where his father had a big ranch. I am very appreciative of all he showed me, and always will be. Frankie was a friend and mentor to me, and I owe him so much.

People always ask me what different promoters are like, and it's hard to answer. I found all of them the same really, more or less. As long as you made them money, they treated you right. For me, I always gave it everything I had, and the fans loved me or hated me, depending on how I was trying to get over. Von Erich was no different, but after a few months I left for the Carolinas. The Von Erichs were very good promoters, and while I was there, the Sheik and I trained his sons. They were very good kids. It's a shame what happened to that family over the years—they have had to go through so much pain from too many tragedies. David died in Japan, while Michael, Chris, and Kerry all committed suicide. It is very sad. Kevin is the only one still alive. I wrestled with him for a few years, and he is a good man.

Although I wasn't in Texas for long, I made the most of my time there. Gino Hernandez teamed with me to win the NWA Texas tag team titles, beating Bruiser Brody and Mike York. We held the belts for only a short time, though, before dropping the gold. Belts never meant much to me. What good are belts when you have to lose them to someone else?

Texas was a short stay for me, and I continued to move around. For a few years, I worked for Jim Barnett in Georgia Championship Wrestling. I teamed with Gordy for a while and won some gold belts with him, but I moved on shortly after that because the Crockett brothers wanted me for their Mid-Atlantic Wrestling organization in Charlotte, North Carolina. Jim Crockett paid more than Don Owens, and he paid me on time every night after every show. I really liked it there. My family and I moved to Charlotte and stayed nearly three years. By then, it was me, my mom, Sharon, and our three kids. Sharon and I had two daughters after Jimmy Jr.—Liana "Louise" Frances Reiher Snuka in 1974, and Sarona Moana-Marie Reiher Snuka in 1978. We didn't have a perfect marriage, but we had a nice family. To be honest, brudda, the marriage was terrible. Sharon and I fought all the time. I want to make clear that I only pushed her away to keep her from hitting me. I would never use full force. I don't like confrontation. I didn't take good care of my responsibilities, but I did make sure my family was okay financially. I was so happy the kids were able to come to my matches. My way of saying hello to them was by pinching my nose before I entered the ring. As my children got older, Sharon told them stories about me that were not flattering, and for a long time it kept me apart from my children.

> "Growing up in a household that was always on the move taught me to adjust quickly to new surroundings and to always stay close to my family. Not seeing my father for months at a time was hard, but when he did come home it made up for all the days missed. We were taught that family is everything and that we stick together, no matter what! I would best describe my childhood as a great path of stepping stones that made me who I've become today. I would never change any of it."
> —Sarona Snuka-Polamalu, Timmy's daughter and WWE Diva

Many wrestlers seemed to follow me from each territory. For example, I told The Iron Sheik to come to Portland before I moved on from there. Just as Frankie Laine did for me all those years ago, I talked up Sheik to Don Owens. I told him Sheik was from Iran and was a very good worker. I also told Sheik to start wearing those famous boots with the toes curled up, because it felt real. Sheik was so skilled, and with his gimmick, he was the total package. He was an Olympic champion wrestler, and he knew all the real Olympic wrestling moves.

When Sheik got to Portland, the first thing I did was drop my belt to him to get him over. I always did stuff like that, because I wanted what was best for the story and the company—not just what was best for me. I was getting paid either way, so who cared if I won or lost a match? All that mattered was that I delivered a great performance.

Ricky "The Dragon" Steamboat was another brudda I told to come wrestle with me—only that was in Mid-Atlantic. Ricky Steamboat was a face in the Carolinas and I was a heel. It was awesome. I liked to play a heel, because I was in control. Whenever I went to a new territory, I was always the heel at first, and then turned face. Me and Ricky, the two of us in the ring in Charlotte, were just magic, brudda. It was genius against genius in the ring. He wanted it, and I wanted it. We went into the ring, and it was just like, "Let's go, brah!" I beat him for the NWA United States title in North Carolina. I got many other wrestlers, including Ricky, to enter bodybuilding competitions with me. It was just fun for us to get away and flex. I actually came in second to Ricky at one competition. I was happy for him, brudda! Tony Atlas was also there, and it was a lot of fun. We worked damn hard in the gym to get our bodies looking like that. We were all buff and just totally ripped. We loved showing off and not having to beat up on each other.

> "He probably had some influence on me entering some competitions. He had already won a competition. I won, but it was only because I was more cut up, and he was smooth. He had these huge Polynesian calves. I was just more ripped. It was that close. I was a babyface and he was the heel, so maybe the fan response was for me because I was a good guy."
> —Ricky "The Dragon" Steamboat

I can't say enough about Ricky. I just loved being around him. He was so good at what he did. He had natural instincts in the ring and this amazing body. He worked hard to be the best, just like I did. When we wrestled a match, we knew exactly what we were doing without even saying a word to each other.

"That's a special treat, when you get in a ring and do some stuff without talking about it. Or when you do talk about it, you don't even have to finish your sentence. I would start, and Jimmy would go, 'I got the rest of it, brother. Don't worry.' Somehow we just knew each other. God, his body language was so intense, but it was like working with air. I liked the initial contact to be solid. It looked like he was ripping you apart, but you didn't feel him. And he had such spring in his legs. He was doing springboards before the word was even invented. He was like, 'I just jump off the apron from the top and hit you with a cross body or clothesline or something else.' He was doing stuff like that before the terminology was even invented."
—Ricky "The Dragon" Steamboat

I also had some great matches with Ric Flair. He was a really good worker. I didn't get to know him really well, because he was a face when I was a heel. We had to keep up the appearances of the show, you know? So, when we went out to a bar after an event, the faces were on one side of the bar, and the heels were on the other side.

Paul Orndorff was another good worker in the ring. He was a lot like me, in that he worked out all the time, played sports, and had an amazing body. We worked out together a lot. I was older than Paul and Ricky, so they knew I'd been around and

both would listen and learn. When Paul and I were teamed up, we won the tag team titles in 1979 against Baron von Raschke and Greg "The Hammer" Valentine. Paul was a good kid. He wanted it so bad.

"I was a baby rookie in St. Louis, wrestling for maybe a year, when the Crocketts asked me to team with Jimmy in the Carolinas. I had heard about him. There weren't a lot of Jimmy Snukas around. I knew he'd fly in the ring, and had a hell of a body and a look. I jumped all over that opportunity. Being teamed up with somebody like that every day of the week rubs off on you. Jimmy influenced my career and showed me the right things to do. He taught me how to tell a story in the ring and work together. Things weren't the way they are now in the business. There wasn't an easy way to earn a spot. You earned it by hard work. He was just so good at it. There wasn't anyone better than Jimmy."
—Paul Orndorff, WWE Hall of Famer

WRESTLING IN JAPAN

No matter which promotion I was working with, I always made time to go back to Japan. They always treated me so well there, and the crowds were electric, brah! Some of my best memories are there, brudda. I love those people. Whenever wrestlers went to Japan back in the day, they were treated like kings! Whether it was wrestling Terry and Dory Funk Jr. or Stan Hanson or Terry Gordy—it was always an amazing time there in Japan. I can't say that enough.

> "In the late 1970s and early 1980s, wrestling was just more mainstream in Japan. It was a major sport there compared to a fringe sport. Guys were more recognized everywhere they went. They looked different than anyone, and had that larger-than-life thing since they were on network TV."
> —Dave Meltzer

There were two big Japanese companies that I wrestled for—All Japan Wrestling and New Japan Wrestling—and the fans just ate it up. I'd even say that wrestling was bigger there than it was in the United States, and that's saying something, brudda! My main man while I was wrestling in Japan was Bruiser Brody. He and I were always on the same page, and we had some great matches together as tag team partners. I remember our matches against the Funk Brothers like they were yesterday. Some people said that Bruiser was in it for himself, and that he was hard to work with. He was somewhat like that, but I give him credit. He was a good worker. We learned a lot from one another. Bruiser and Stan Hansen were so stiff, they would just give you a kick when your back was turned. So, you had to be prepared when you worked with those guys. I got many "potatoes" from them when we were in Japan.

Bruiser and I were smart both inside and outside the ring. We worked with promoter Shohei "Giant" Baba and All Japan early on, and we were larger than life in that territory, brudda. The two of us were tag team champs and loved what we did so much. Sometimes it felt like Bruiser Brody and I shared a brain. We didn't take shit from anyone, and the crowd popped every time! I actually remember being around the city more than I do wrestling the matches. Each time we would walk down the street, people would cross to the other side. I guess we must've looked like Godzilla and King Kong coming toward them. They probably believed the storylines we were in and were a little afraid of us.

"Jimmy was one of the few people Frank [Bruiser Brody] would talk about. He was a very private person. When they were in Japan, he always knew Jimmy had his back, and he had Jimmy's. Frank was his own man, but he believed you give the fans what they wanted. He wanted them to leave saying, 'Dang, was that real or not?' All he wanted was to give the audience their money's worth, and make money for everybody. He and Jimmy shared that, and that's why they got along so good together."
—Barbara Goodish, Bruiser Brody's widow

Bruiser and I both eventually changed alliances and left Baba for his former partner, Antonio Inoki, and his New Japan Wrestling. It wasn't an easy decision but we felt we weren't being treated the right way. We were on our way to finish off a tag team tournament in Osaka, but we just got off the train, and that was that. We didn't want to lose, so we just decided to leave. We deserved better. We both felt that way, and I followed Bruiser's lead. After that, Inoki had to protect us from All Japan and its fans. Wrestling was a serious and dangerous business then—even more so in Japan.

"I think Brody had an issue with money. He brokered a deal with Fritz Von Erich to send talent for New Japan, and he was supposed to get a commission. There was more to that, I'm sure. That was a ballsy move. I don't know if it was a good move. They did get to go to All Japan afterward, but leaving the tag team tournament was a big deal. It was probably a year until they were able to go back to Japan to wrestle again. It wasn't like they just went to All Japan the next month. There was a penalty."
—Dave Meltzer

Bruiser and I continued to wrestle in Japan for years. I was there in 1988 waiting for Brody to come back from wrestling in Puerto Rico when Baba sent one of his boys over with some terrible news: Brody had been murdered. I was just in shock. It was all so very sad. Bruiser Brody was a good brudda, I cannot say that enough. He was a hell of a businessman and a great worker. In many ways, I feel like he is underrated in wrestling history. He was one of the good ones. And, like I said, we were of the same mind when it came to wrestling. I miss him so much to this day.

I did eventually leave Mid-Atlantic when Vince Kennedy McMahon Sr. asked me to wrestle for his Northeast promotion, World Wrestling Federation. I was ready to go to the next level.

I was in my thirties, and I had paid my dues in the territories. It was time to take the biggest stage in the States. I knew the fans would love me. I knew I offered something that they had never seen before. And, like I said, I never met a challenge I didn't take head-on. I saw an opportunity and I just jumped at it, brudda. I owed it to myself to go to the biggest city in the world, and the fans were about to see what the Superfly could do.

> "We were owners at Georgia Championship Wrestling—my brother and I—and we wanted Jimmy to stay. We didn't want him going to the WWF. There were several guys we wanted to keep, but Jimmy, being such a free spirit, wanted to work Madison Square Garden and Boston, and who could blame him?"
> —Gerald Brisco

CHAPTER 3

UNDER THE BRIGHT LIGHTS

"Jimmy was in demand by all the territories here in the States. He was a bona fide star everywhere he went, but New York and the WWWF/WWF put him on the professional wrestling map. His style and look was unique, and his in-ring work was incredible. Finally, Jimmy Snuka had arrived in America."
—Mean Gene Okerlund

I was excited to go to New York after Mid-Atlantic. This was the big stage, the biggest territory in the world, and the biggest bucks. I took to Vince McMahon Sr. right away. He was an honest man who I really respected a lot. He wanted to make me the champion there eventually—he told me so. That's not why I went to New York, but it helped. Everything I had done up to that point prepared me to be the biggest star in the biggest city in the world. I had a reputation in the business as a hard worker, an innovative wrestler, and, yes, as a party guy. I've told you already about that—the Superfly loved to party it up, brudda.

I made my debut in the World Wrestling Federation against Barry Hart on March 12, 1982. I was so excited to get to the big city. New York fans are always the best. They are so passionate about the business, and back in the early 1980s, the crowd was just electric, brudda! I felt the fans would really like what I did, so I was surprised the WWF started me as a heel. But I didn't mind it at all. It never mattered to me whether I was a good guy or a bad guy, I always had fun. They gave me Captain Lou Albano as my manager, and he was so nice to me from the start. He was a beautiful man. I remember the first time I was working for the WWF, we were in Charlotte, North Carolina. He came up to me in the locker room and said, "I'm Lou Albano, and I'm going to manage you." From that moment, we just clicked.

My first big feud was with then-WWF champ Bob Backlund, and we had many amazing matches, brudda. Bob was a pro. He was trained by the best, and we told a great story in the ring. The first match I remember I won by disqualification, because Backlund didn't want to release a chokehold he had on me. Madison Square Garden fans went crazy during our next couple of matches. They were cheering me even though I was a heel. That had never happened before, brudda—at least not at that level. I had had fans cheer me as a bad guy in the territories, but not this many people, brudda! The camera flashes just went nuts this time!

"I had gotten a call from Terry and Dory Funk inviting me on a trip to Japan. Right before we went, I get a call from Vince McMahon Sr. He told me, 'Make sure [Jimmy's] at the Garden for the main event,' and asked me to make sure he was on the plane. Here was the most influential man in pro wrestling, and I was babysitting his star.

"I didn't want to go out with Snuka because I'd been told he was a wild man. However, one night I went out to a karaoke bar, and Snuka was there with Haku and Terry Funk. Karaoke bars were new back then. Snuka asked me to sing. I'm a showman—a professional singer—so I sang 'My Way' by Frank Sinatra. Snuka applauded and took me to two or three more places. That was a lot of fun.

"But every night when I was out with him, I kept hearing Vince Sr.'s voice in my head. So, we're leaving Japan, and we stop in Hawaii. Snuka tells me he has a lot of friends there, and he wants to take me out. So, he takes me to this luau with hundreds of people there. What I didn't know was that a hula girl was going to pick me out in the audience to dance with. Jimmy was going out with that young girl probably, and they went out drinking afterward. I was at the Waikiki Circle Hotel, and I decided I just wanted to sit out on the porch. I went to bed at 1:00 AM, and I see him through the window, and he's clearly drunk. He looked like one of those actors who played the crazed Indians in the old Westerns after they had too much whiskey. I just didn't want any part of him. An hour or so later, I hear somebody banging on doors outside and screaming, 'Brudda Bill!' I open the door, and he's stark naked screaming, 'Where is she?' I said, 'What are you talking about?' He was asking for that girl. So, he goes onto the balcony and he's yelling out her name from nine stories up. He ended up falling asleep on the balcony, and here I am looking at this naked savage, hearing Vince Sr.'s voice in my head.

"He wound up in one of the two beds in my room. I couldn't wake him up the next morning, so I left for the airport alone. There was no Internet back then, so I'm trying to collect call Vince Sr. long distance. Snuka comes to me five minutes before the plane is about to take off. He says to me, 'I never knew you could dance like that,' like nothing happened. We wound up at the Garden, and Snuka had his first match with Bob Backlund."
—Bill Apter

On June 28, 1982, which was a little while after Vince McMahon Jr. purchased the company from his father, I had a match with Backlund in a steel cage at Madison Square Garden that is still one of the matches I'm most known for. The crowd was popping, brudda! Now, some people think my steel cage match with Don Muraco was the first time I climbed to the top of the cage, but it was not. I had done it with The Iron Sheik before back in the Portland days, and I did it with Backlund that night.

By the time I wrestled Backlund, I had done it a few times, but that was the first time so many people were seeing it. Vince Sr. had wanted me to win the belt that night but I thought it'd make a better story if Backlund beat me that night and I beat him the next. It was my idea for Backlund to win the match—for him to move out of the way when I jumped from the top of the cage. Unfortunately, I never got a chance to take on Backlund and win the belt. The opportunity never came, but I still remember that one match. The two of us got it just right. We talked during the entire match, and planned when we would hit our spots. It was easy.

"I wrestled him numerous times. I remember we wrestled July 10, 1982, in Maryland, for the first time. I was down in Florida, Amarillo, and St. Louis, and I believe he was in the Carolina territories. I didn't know him from Adam. But I saw he was very skillful in creating a match in the ring. It was not about good guys or bad guys—it developed during the match. He was very adroit at that. I think this is the way wrestling should be learned. You learn to have a match first, not how to make a character. Once you learn how to work the crowd, then you work character. Jimmy listened to the crowd, and had a lot of patience. I got to be in the ring with a lot of people, and he was as good as anyone at telling a story."

—*Bob Backlund*

Backlund was a pro to work with. He was this very humble man who was right out of college. When we were planning the match, it didn't go long. We both understood the business. He was a good worker, and always stayed out of trouble. Drugs were everywhere, but Backlund always walked the straight line. He didn't want any part of that. He wrestled for the love of wrestling. He didn't care about the drugs and stuff. He was a good worker, and you have got to respect that about him. Backlund was skilled and focused on wrestling, and he never let anything get in the way of that.

"I remember that cage match very well. It was a unique one. I didn't really like cage matches. I liked wrestling 30 minutes, an hour, and having some art to it. I liked when we didn't have to have any other gimmicks. It showed more skill. But it's one of my most memorable matches. He was quite a fantastic athlete, and when he climbed up to the top of the cage, and I moved out of the way, and crawled out of the cage, it was a very memorable thing."
—Bob Backlund

I just wanted to climb to the top of the cage and give fans something to freak out about, to show them something they'd never seen before. Even though I didn't hit the splash on Backlund, that match led to me turning face, because the fans were cheering me so much.

> "Even in New York, they couldn't keep him as a heel.
> The people just cheered him. They just refused to
> boo him. He was over so strong."
> —*Rowdy Roddy Piper, WWE Hall of Famer*

> "Mick Foley, Bubba Ray Dudley, and I were all there—not
> together—when Jimmy famously jumped off the steel cage
> against Don Muraco. I was also there the first time he did it at the
> Garden against Bob Backlund and missed. That was so unheard
> of. Jimmy was such a vicious, vicious heel, and I only liked the
> good guys. But when he turned—pile-driven by Ray Stevens on
> the concrete floor—I remember going crazy about that."
> —*Tommy Dreamer*

The idea they came up with was having Lou Albano turn on me. We were at Buddy Rogers' Corner, and the storyline was that Lou stole money from me. People really believed it, brudda. When Lou and Ray Stevens turned against me, the fans just loved it. Lou and I were so hot back in the day. I know those matches don't get talked about today, but I loved working with Lou in the ring, brudda. I'll say this about the Captain—he was a very good wrestler but an even better manager. He always wanted me to splash him, but he was my manager, so I couldn't. When I turned face, I did get to splash him, and he loved it. He said, "You were smooth!" I hit him and bounced off that brudda and had to crawl back to pin him down.

"Jimmy was the man in the WWF, from his run with Backlund to turning babyface. He was the main reason people were going to Madison Square Garden."
—Tommy Dreamer

Some of my favorite WWF matches, though, were with Ray Stevens. I remember juicing so much for those pile drivers I took from Ray. During one match, he gave me a pile driver on the concrete, and the crowd exploded for it. I really sold that one, brudda. I remember blading during the match just to sell it. I've juiced ever since I started in the business. Men with guts did it. I wouldn't tell the promoters or the wrestlers when I was going to do it, just to keep them on their toes. I'd cut my forehead, my chest, my arms—it didn't matter. And I've got the scars to prove it, brudda. During those matches with Stevens, an ambulance would pick me up at the hotel and bring me to the Garden to hide me. Ray Stevens was such a good brudda. He taught me so much. I was lucky to have people like him around to help me.

On the other hand, Lou told me he didn't trust Buddy Rogers. I had cut that promo with Lou on Rogers' show, when Buddy told me on TV that Lou spent my money. The funny thing was that on camera, Lou was the bad guy and Buddy was telling me not to trust him. In reality, Buddy was the one I shouldn't have trusted. He was just riding my boat to success. Watch him as I walk into the ring during the cage match against Muraco. He's in his suit, just following me to get noticed. He wiggled his way into becoming my manager. Years later, he became my neighbor in New Jersey, and I believe he had an affair with Sharon. I also think he bashed me to people and said I got her hooked on drugs. But I didn't force Sharon to take drugs. We just did them together. But I was responsible for bringing the drugs into our home.

Back in those days, people thought what was happening on television was actually happening in real life. One time, I remember Lou wanted to walk down the beach on our way to the arena. As we were strolling along, I looked and said, "Brudda El Captain, do you see what is going on?" People started to notice us! They began to yell curse words at Lou, telling him to leave me alone. "Jimmy is a good guy, and you are no good!" they said. I told Lou we needed to leave right away. Lou really took a beating from the fans. They would slash his tires, and he was even cut once by a fan.

There will never be another Captain Lou. He loved to drink a gallon of vodka after an event. Vince Sr. would be there, and Lou would bring his gallon with him to eat. He took it everywhere he went—that was his gimmick. He never drank before an event, but he made up for it afterward. He was a good guy, and didn't fool around like some of the guys did. He took his job seriously.

I continued to wrestle many of the all-time greats. It was really the golden age of wrestling, and I felt so lucky to be a part of it. I had matches against Superstar Billy Graham, and teamed up with my longtime friend Andre the Giant. Together, we took on many top teams, including The Wild Samoans. I used to love jumping off Andre's shoulders during those matches. Andre was as solid a guy as there ever was. We had full trust in each other. Freddie Blassie was not my manager, but I knew him and he was just lovely to be around. I was so lucky to be with guys like Albano, Blassie, and so many others. You learned something different every day from somebody. It was a new school for me. I'd meet all these veterans, and I was forced to listen. I didn't have a choice. It's not like I could read up on anything.

> "We weren't surprised Jimmy became a wrestling star. We thought he'd end up becoming a movie star like our cousin, The Rock. The Rock got his eyebrow thing from Jimmy, by the way..."
> —Louise Reiher

PERSONAL DEMONS

I was continuing to perform to sold-out crowds after my feuds with Albano, Stevens, and others. But in 1983, my personal life started getting a little crazy. I always loved to party. I loved to drink, brudda, and during that year, I was doing a lot of cocaine. I had been for a year by then.

There were a lot of drugs in New York City in the 1980s, and I started using them after I'd been there a little while. I never did cocaine until I got to New York. *Io*—that's Fijian for "yes"—drugs were always around the Superfly on the road, but I chose

to drink and chase ladies instead. I didn't want anything getting in the way of my wrestling. But everything changed in New York. The temptation was just too much for me. I started using steroids a lot, because they were right there for all of us, brudda. That didn't make it right, but it was just so easy to get them. I thought it was all part of the program. What did I know? Not much. I thought it was medicine for the wrestlers. There was a doctor in the locker room—George Zahorian—and he gave us the pills. He ended up going to jail for doing this later on. What he was doing was illegal, but I didn't know that. Once I found out what they were, I could've stopped taking them, but I didn't. I got greedy. I wanted to get bigger and bigger, even though I was already a good size. But steroids weren't my biggest problem.

"Vince McMahon will tell you to this day he worked the guys way too hard. With the day-to-day grind—and I'm not excusing it—shit gets out of hand, and you're in the middle of it, and everything around you is spinning."
—Don Muraco, WWE Hall of Famer

It took some time to get into the drugs. Again, for years in Portland, I never even thought about taking them. I just went about my business and did some pot and drank a lot. In my first couple of months in New York, I was still not interested. After a while, I started wanting more out of my life in New York, and it became all too easy to find drugs. So, the Superfly tried cocaine. I was feeling down. I was feeling like I was not being used right, so maybe I just wanted to feel good. All I remember is that everyone wanted to party with the Superfly. They still do, brudda! Back in New York, we would go to a party or we would go to a bar after a match. Didn't matter. We went wherever the drugs were.

I never injected drugs in my body. I didn't like the idea of needles going into my veins. At first, I didn't like cocaine either. The first time I tried it, I remember being egged on to snort more and more. I felt quite a rush the first time I tried coke, but not in a good way. It was like an out-of-body experience. I like to be in control of my body at all times, so cocaine was a real shock to my body and my mind. The Superfly didn't like it. I just stood there and questioned why everyone did cocaine when it made you feel so messed up. I remember telling myself I'd never take it again. I didn't at first, but then I'd get drunk at the next party and start doing cocaine again. Eventually, it started feeling good. It made me very comfortable, and I'm not going to lie, sometimes it took away the pain from all the bumps I took in the ring.

I had bad experiences with the police in 1983, too. It was just the worst year ever, brudda. I was waiting for a title shot, doing drugs all the time, drinking with the boys, and continuing to party with all the girls—and then it all came crashing down. It started one night at our hotel in Oneida, New York, near Syracuse. Us boys would always stay at a hotel that had a bar downstairs so we could eat and drink and not have to drive anywhere. Then, we would go up to our rooms, get up the next day, and be on the road again.

> "Jimmy was an A-list partier. He was just as wild outside the ring as he was inside the ring. If you're going to party with Jimmy Snuka, you had to be prepared to party for 30 hours, be up the next morning to catch a plane, and be ready the next night to perform, because he certainly was. He was one of those brothers who wouldn't turn anybody down, because he thought it was disrespectful. So, you'd walk into a bar, and he'd order a couple rounds, and then before you knew it, everybody at the place bought him a round. Before you knew it, he'd have 10 beers around him."
> —Gerald Brisco

I was not doing coke that night, just drinking a lot of booze, as were a lot of the other guys in the room. The beer was everywhere, and the women were all over the place. For me, it was just me and my "friend" on the side. I say friend, but she was really my girlfriend. I was not faithful to Sharon at all when I was on the road, and Nancy Argentino understood that. She was my East Coast girlfriend. We were drinking and having a good time when all of a sudden, the police burst into our room. I don't know why they chose my room—maybe mine was the first one they passed—but they did. It was not just one cop, brudda. It was six men in blue with police dogs and everything. I remember asking them what the problem was. I was in my underwear, and they were all confrontational. They beat me up with their batons. Now, I'm not saying I was totally innocent in all this—I was pretty drunk—but after a while I was just protecting myself from getting beaten. They had busted down the door of my room and were poking me in the balls with their night sticks, and I was not going to let anyone poke me in the balls.

Apparently, the manager at the front desk was getting angry calls from the other hotel guests, complaining that we were being too loud. When one guest said she heard screaming, saw women walking around the hall naked, and that someone was possibly getting beaten, the manager called the cops. I don't know anything about that. I never laid my hands on anyone, and I didn't see any naked women, aside from the one in my room. Nancy was screaming at the cops when they came into our room. I was so angry. I didn't need to be handcuffed with German shepherds barking at me. I was drinking some beer, and maybe smoking some pot. But that was it.

I remember they yelled at me to put my clothes on so they could take me to jail. I refused. I don't mind being in my underwear—I wrestle in tights, brudda! To this day, I'll mow the lawn in a Speedo. They hauled me out in my underwear and took me to prison. I tried to explain to them that we were just having fun and apologized for waking people up. Again, I was in my room with Nancy, and the boys were the ones partying and making all kinds of noise. I ended up pleading guilty just to get it over with. I did not assault Nancy—she was fine. I went back to the hotel to get our clothing and the car, and then I went back to the station to get Nancy. And just like that, we were on our way to the next event.

There were a lot of us there—I don't know why they singled me out. I mean, I was the biggest draw at the time, but I don't think they knew that. In the end, I paid a fine, and the charges were dropped.

ABOUT NANCY ARGENTINO

I've said it before—life on the road could get very lonely, so the boys would always go out and party. Partying usually meant going out for drinks, doing cocaine at a house or a hotel room, and sleeping with some girl you either just met or had on the side. Many of us had women in each part of the world. I met Nancy Argentino at a show. She was a fan and had been friends with another wrestler named Johnny Rodz.

Nancy quickly became a friend I'd see whenever I was on the East Coast. We slept together each time, but we also hung out. She was a very nice girl, and we got along right way. She understood our arrangement. For maybe six months or a year, we spent a lot of time together. One afternoon, we were driving to Allentown, Pennsylvania—just she and I—from a Connecticut show because I had a TV shoot the next morning. We were drinking some beers, and she asked me to stop so that she could pee. I pulled over to the side of the road and I waited in the car for her, drinking. When she came back, she told me she slipped on the way and hit her head. I didn't see it happen, but I remember she told me she was jumping over a little river or stream that was there and she slipped. She seemed okay, and when I asked her if she was feeling all right, she said yes. I didn't see any blood anywhere, so neither of us was concerned and we kept driving to Allentown.

> "I met Nancy once in the dressing room. What was unusual about her was that her hair was styled exactly like Jimmy's. It was almost scary. She was beautiful, but looked like him."
> —Bill Apter

I think we stopped drinking after that—she did, at least. I asked her over the next few hours if she was feeling better, and she just kept telling me she had a headache. When we finally got to Allentown and checked into our hotel, I told her to lie down and rest. I left her alone for a little bit to hang out with Mr. Fuji and the boys, and she was sleeping when I came back. She seemed fine, so I went to bed.

The next morning, I got up and headed out for the TV shoot. She was still breathing, and I was not concerned that this was a life-or-death situation. At worst, I thought she might have a concussion, and I figured I'd take her to the doctor if she needed to go when I got back. When I got back to the hotel, I remember being very surprised that she was still in bed. I woke her up, but she could hardly breathe. I called the front desk, and asked them to call an ambulance. I followed the ambulance to the hospital. Two hours later, they told me she had passed away. I think she died of a fracture to her skull. I was devastated.

At the funeral, I told her mother and father how sorry I was about her death. What else could I possibly say? I just remember telling them I was very sorry and that I cared for her. I went to the church with them, and their daughter was there in a coffin, and I just said I wish it hadn't happened. I had no reason to hurt her. They didn't accuse me of anything. I heard stories that I threatened Nancy's sister at one point. I never did that. That is not true.

Shortly after Nancy's death, I was questioned by police and let go. At one point, I went with Vince McMahon Jr. to either a court or law office, I don't remember which because I was still in shock. All I remember is he had a briefcase with him. I don't know what happened. I think Vince Jr. picked me up from the hotel and took me there. He didn't say anything to me. I don't know if he gave Nancy's family money or anything. The only thing I know for sure is that I didn't hurt Nancy. I couldn't believe what had happened. Some people have written that I was just playing stupid, but I really didn't know what was happening around me.

"It was the same night of Eddie Gilbert's accident, when his Lincoln Continental hit an 18-wheeler, and I was there. I was at the hospital all night. The next morning, the homicide detectives got to the hotel. They were knocking on Jimmy's door, and I guess he was confused or was not understanding who they were, so I spoke to them, and they informed me Nancy had passed away the night before. I spoke to Jimmy, and called Vince Jr. to tell him what was going on with Eddie Gilbert and Jimmy. He jumped in a car, drove to Allentown, and that was it. I had no part in any meetings or anything. It was just three weeks after the promo where we went at it, when I spit at Snuka and he tore off my clothes and hit me with a microphone."
—Don Muraco

Many terrible things have been written about me hurting Nancy and being responsible for her death, but they are not true. This has been very hard on me and very hard on my family. To this day, I get nasty notes and threats. It hurts. I never hit Nancy or threatened her. I never wanted to harm her. That day she fell on the concrete, we didn't do drugs together—we just drank. I'm not saying we never did drugs together, but that day we just drank together and were having a good time. She fell by accident, and I didn't realize how bad she was hurt. I feel terrible that I didn't get her checked out by a doctor sooner.

I felt really bad, and it's been hard every day since. I've had a lot of support from my family over the years—even Sharon was a little supportive, despite the fact I had cheated on her. She did want me to take some time off to be with our family.

I will say this about the whole thing, brudda—that night ruined my life. To this day, that is how I feel. If I was guilty of anything, it was cheating on my wife, and that was it. I love women. I enjoy them. I respect them. I love the smell of the ladies. I would never hurt any of them. Nancy was a good girl. I will never forget what happened to her.

"It affected [his legacy]. People romanticize him a lot. I don't think it tainted his career, though. I think there was an awareness about it. It was covered in the paper, but it wasn't like big headlines—not like how it is today with TMZ. It's not like fans would go out to the arenas and boo him. People wanted to like him. He was a natural babyface. He just stood out everywhere. I remember the [arrest] with the dogs more. There was follow-up in the papers on that one."
—Dave Meltzer

DECONSTRUCTING THE MATCH WITH "MAGNIFICENT" DON MURACO

Don Muraco and I had a major feud in the WWF later in 1983. He was the Intercontinental Champion, and I was making a run for that belt. I had won the first match, but it was by disqualification, so it didn't bring me the gold. Whenever Don and I locked up, it was gold, brudda. His pile driver was a great move. I don't remember him ever putting it on me, but I have seen him do it so many times. It's a very dangerous move—you can break someone's neck if you're not careful. Both men have to work together on that move. I let the Undertaker give me the pile driver years later because I trusted him, and because he is a very good wrestler. I don't let just anyone give me the pile driver.

Anyway, Don and I had known each other since the early 1970s back in Hawaii, and we wrestled each other so many times that by the time we ended up at WWF together, we were in total sync. He was and remains a good friend of mine. His wife's name is Sharon, so I would always call her "Sister." We all got along good. We would have barbecues together, whether it was at his house or mine. I would also surf with Don on the North Shore of Hawaii. Don still likes to surf to this day. The two of us had great respect for each other, and just loved working against each other and working the crowd. We were so damn hot back then.

> "The biggest feuds, sometimes the greatest matches, are the ones that people say, 'God, those guys really hated each other.' Jimmy and I were of the same mind-set. Me and Jimmy, Bruno Sammartino and Harley Race—guys like that, you generally know the other guy as well as you know yourself. That trust and selflessness leads to a lot of the better performances, if you're physically capable."
>
> —Don Muraco

I took my mom to Madison Square Garden when I jumped off the top of the steel cage against Don Muraco on October 17, 1983. My whole family was there. I remember my wife and daughters were wearing fur coats I had bought for them. My mother didn't know what I planned to do that night, but Don Muraco and I did.

I remember our cage match like it was yesterday, brudda. Madison Square Garden was sold out. Flashbulbs were going off like crazy. Don Muraco entered the ring first, and he was just going nuts out there, brudda. He had come out with Captain Lou, and Lou was doing his thing outside the ring before he was told to go back to the locker room. Man, Lou knew how to work the crowd. Inside the ring before I came in, Don was just so pumped up. He was like, "C'mon, let's get it on!" He couldn't wait for me to come out. We hadn't really prepared the match beforehand—we may have taken a few minutes to discuss the outcome, but in the ring, we would set out to do what we always did: tell a great story.

> **"There's only one reason why it has come to this kind of conclusion. Don Muraco...you know it, and I know it. The only reason why we're in this situation, brudda, in a steel cage, is because you know what you did. It started off with Lou Albano... it comes on and on, now's it's up to you...Nobody forgets deep down inside when somebody does something wrong to them... Just remember, tonight, believe me, anything can happen...The steel cage is for two animals to go in there..."**
> —Jimmy "Superfly" Snuka promo prior to Don Muraco match

Buddy Rogers escorted me out to the ring, and like I said, he was just riding my coattails. He had fancy suits and a nice look about him so he got over with the crowd, but everyone was there to see me. I remember watching the match recently and someone was holding a sign that said, "When Snuka Flies, Muraco Dies." I loved that.

I remember walking around the ring and just looking up at the cage. I slowly made my way in the ring, and brudda, the best part was when I got in and started locking up with Don. The fans were electric, and we built it up and up. We took our time, brah. We were just cruising—taking it one step at a time. We checked each other out first, and then we went for it.

You have to go slowly. That tells the story, and allows you the time to figure out what the fans are expecting next. I started off with some chops, and Don sold them. We were dancers in there. But we were also listening to the crowd and having fun the whole time. The whole time, we were choreographing where we were going. I was like, "C'mon, brudda, kick me right in the gut!" When he threw me into the steel cage, I quickly juiced my forehead. They don't bleed in wrestling much today—they don't know how to, and they don't know when. It's all in the timing. Don threw me into the cage, and I sold it, brudda.

We talked through every move. When we both started climbing the cage together, it was all planned—so was the ending. I knew I'd give Don a head butt, and he would go flying out the cage door and win the match. It was just perfect. Again, I was never a glory guy. I didn't care about the belt. I cared about telling a good story in the ring and making everyone who paid their money to see the match happy. So, when Muraco won, I sold it that I was going cuckoo. I was screaming, "No way!" I didn't want it to end, brah. I took Muraco and put him back in the cage. The match was not over yet!

I picked him up and suplexed him, and Muraco made sure he was in the center of the ring. I looked up at the cage and started climbing the wall. Later, when I watched the match on tape, I loved how Gorilla Monsoon called it, saying the place was going "bananas." They really were, bruddas! It was just like the time I tried to splash Backlund when I was a heel, only better. Now I was a face, and I was about to do something that had never been done before. So, I climbed up, and I splashed him. But again, I did it right and I did it slow. I protected Don with my arms and my knees, and Don kept his arms up and slowly lifted himself off the mat.

"Muraco was a heel who could wrestle, brawl, fly, cut incredible promos, and do it all. And then there was Jimmy Snuka. His leap off the top rope at the time was as great a move as had ever been seen. And on that memorable night at MSG in 1983 when everything magically came together—two warriors in their prime, in a feud that mattered, in a cage to boot—there was electricity in the air. I know, because I was there. As Muraco lay there prone in the middle of the ring, Snuka climbed to the top of the steel cage.

"'No, no, he isn't going to do it...' I said excitedly to my best buddy, Scott, as Snuka stood on top of the cage. 'No! No way!' he responded in amazement. But that was exactly what Jimmy was about to do. And as he perched upright on the cage for what felt like forever, the excitement reached a crescendo. Then he made his leap, remarkably first springing upward, even higher than the cage itself.

> **"It may have been the most incredible moment in the history of pro wrestling. The belt—who won—means little these many years later. What is remembered is that leap."**
> —*Evan Ginzburg, associate producer of* The Wrestler

I was like a bird ready to land, and he came up to catch me, so we broke the fall together. If I landed flat on top of him—forget it. But we had it down pat. Afterward, I stood up and threw the belt on him and dropped down on one knee. The crowd ate it up. I remember when Don and I got back to the locker room, we were on such a high. It was such a rush having that match, and we were so happy. We worked hard, and the locker room was quiet. The other boys just watched us walking in. What could they have said?

> **"I'll never forget that night he jumped off the cage. You still see film of it. It was a 'holy shit' moment. That has to rank in the top 10 of the thousands of WWE moments. It was the first time you'd ever seen a human being jump off the cage and onto another human lying in the ring. I mean, you want to talk about trust? Everybody has to be on the same page for that. Jimmy could've overshot him by six inches and driven a knee into Muraco's ribs. I've taken many of those Snuka splashes. He breaks his fall with his knees and elbows, but it's got to be perfect. He'd always say, 'Trust me, brudda.'"**
> —*Ricky "The Dragon" Steamboat*

When my mom met me after the match, she said, "You rascal," because she didn't know I was going to jump off the cage. No one in my family knew I was going to do it. That's how it was back in the day. Nothing was told to anyone. My kids were also there, and they had no clue about what I was going to do. The video of that moment plays on WWE TV even today, and people watch it on YouTube, but I can tell you, it was just something I did. I had already tried the top rope, so I figured, why not the top of the cage? No one else was doing it, so why couldn't I? I didn't even give it a thought, brudda.

> "I remember we went to the Don Muraco [steel cage] match, and how he came out and the way he was. I remember just watching him and being like, 'That's my dad!' Back in those days, wrestling was kept secret—nobody knew how it was going to be. Even to us, we didn't know. I remember at the Muraco match crying because I thought my dad was getting hurt."
> —Liana Snuka, *Jimmy's daughter*

It doesn't matter how old I am—I know I could still pull off a splash now. I believe that with every inch of my body, brudda. I know I could climb up to the top of the steel cage again and get things done. I know I can have the fans cheer for me like they once did. I know I could fly at Madison Square Garden, brudda! If the price is right, I'd love to do it again, but it's got to be the right guy. Maybe my nephew, The Rock, would get in the ring with this brudda?

> "It opened another door to a new era. Things were turning right before Hulk Hogan and the commercialization of the WWF. It wasn't just a local phenomenon. It was kind of international. That match, that whole feud, pretty much defined a good portion of our careers."
> —Don Muraco

TAKING DRUGS AND "NOT TONIGHT, BRUDDAS"

That Muraco match capped off a terrible year for me. It was a seesaw year, brudda. After the lovely steel cage match, I started hoping I'd get to be the main guy in the company, but they had other plans for me. My drug use—plus being pissed off at Vince Jr. for not giving me the status I felt I deserved—made me skip out on some matches. I also saw other guys getting paid more than me, and I resented that, brudda. I remember cutting out of shows and letting down my fans because I wanted to go party instead. It was not always like that, though. I liked to have a good time, but I owned up to my responsibilities, too. Still, Vinnie (I always called Vince by that name) was always worried about my behavior, so he'd have someone in the car with me at all times to make sure I arrived on time or at all. But I remember there were times when we would pull up to the building, and I'd be so pissed at something, I'd just say, "Not tonight, bruddas." And I'd refuse to get out of the car.

> "When he was main-eventing everywhere and he just wouldn't show up, it was hard for Vince to keep putting money into him. I got put into some of his matches, and it was hard for me. They'd announce at the last minute that Jimmy wasn't there that night, I'd come in, and get booed for the first 10 minutes. I was his replacement, and they booed the shit out of me. I couldn't blame them. People wanted to see him."
> —Tito Santana, WWE Hall of Famer

There was a lot of destruction in the business, and I was at the center of it. Some people say I did drugs to fit in, but it was just hard to turn the drugs down when they were all around me.

And there was a lot to celebrate when I was working in New York. I was thrown in the main events right away and I drew instant pops from the crowd from the very moment I started. But like I said, there were times I was in another country instead of being in the States, and Vinnie would try to track me down. Many people lied for me, but Vinnie started to use me less and less after that. I knew I was wrong to skip out on matches, but I was angry. Looking back, it's hard to know who was most at fault. On one hand, they promised I would be the main guy in the company, and then Hulk Hogan got all the attention. On the other hand, I had plenty of baggage of my own.

> "I always had a lot of respect for Mr. Snuka in the ring, but I didn't hear so many positive things outside of the ring. I think we were in Buffalo, and I wouldn't let him in my car. I was so very scared he had something in his bag, and if we were pulled over... mentally, I couldn't take that. I had made a lot of promises. Young people have always been very important to me, and I was very protective of my active life, and living up to what I said I was."
> —Bob Backlund

I don't blame Bob for not letting me in his car. I get it. Like I said, I've been a bad boy trying to be a good man my whole life. Besides not showing up to matches and being out of the state and sometimes out of the country when Vinnie needed me, I was arrested a few times because of the drugs and some other unfortunate things I did. Before I quit the WWF, my last arrest was in 1985 when I got caught with cocaine during a tour of the Middle East. I had some coke in a small change purse in my pocket—it was not taped to me as some people have said—and

I was arrested at the airport. I guess I thought I was invincible and I could get away with it. I was not, and I was taken to court and then put in this tiny cell with sand all over the place. It was a dirt hut, and I remember there was one guy in there who was really quiet. I was in that cell for a few hours before Rocky Johnson bailed me out, and that was it. I think I was let out because I was honest about the drugs right away. I do know my status as a wrestling star probably helped me out more. It was not the first time Rocky bailed me out. No, brudda. The Superfly has gotten into trouble quite a bit.

"[One time] he got in a fight in the hotel with one of the Arabs, and he got arrested and went to jail. I was good friends with the King, and I sent for him. The two of us went down and bailed Jimmy out. On the second tour to Arabia, I went two weeks ahead for publicity, because the rest of guys would come in two weeks later. At the airport, Jimmy got caught with drugs. They arrested him and put him in jail. Again I had to go get the King. The King asked, 'Is this going to happen on every tour?' And I answered, 'I hope not.' So, the King and I went and got him out of jail. It was a six-week tour. The King would send his servants over to pick me up in the morning. During the tour the King gave me a Rolex, and I asked if he had one for my brother Jimmy. We have no idea what happened to his Rolex. Jimmy said, 'Ain't no big deal, brudda.'"
—Rocky Johnson

I know I had my share of problems, but I really felt like I was on my way to being the top attraction of WWF. I had been promised by Vince Sr. that I'd be winning the title, but once Vince Jr. took over, I was left waiting for that moment to come. It never did. I

My brudda, Rocky Johnson, and me

think it all comes down to jealousy on Vinnie's part. (I think I'm the only one that's allowed to call him that, by the way.) Listen, before I get into all this, I love Vinnie. He's one of the boys. He works hard, and he's always been good at providing for me and my family. But the bottom line is Vinnie and his father had different opinions of where I was going. I think it all came down to one conversation I had with Vinnie, Vince Sr., and Andre the Giant. The old man was there, and he was telling his son to take care of us. He said to treat us all well. I guess Vince Sr. knew he had cancer by this time and was dying. I didn't know. I was probably the last person to find out. But I remember one thing Vince Sr. told his son that probably made him mad. Vince Sr. told Vinnie to take care of me because he "loved me like a son." I think Vince didn't like that. I've heard he wasn't close with his father growing up, and after hearing his dad say that, I think he was jealous. I felt a shift after that, brudda. One Saturday after that, I called Vince Sr. to just say hello, and his wife told me he was dying. Still, he took the call. I was so upset, but I was happy he picked up the phone. I thanked him for what he had done for me, and said, "I love you and God bless you." He died soon after that conversation. I was so sad when he died. When he told you something, brudda, you know he meant it. He'd look at you, and you knew he was there for you. He kept his promises.

> "Jimmy's role changed when he came to New York. Decisions were made, then in comes [Hulk Hogan], and that was it. It's really hard to explain what the road was like back then. It was lawless, and Jimmy was losing it. I think he thought there was some disrespect. I think he was mad because he was taken advantage of. He didn't do anything wrong in his mind. They made a corporate decision, and Jimmy was going downhill. He could've easily had another four-year run in New York."
> —Rowdy Roddy Piper

I think Vinnie punished me a bit because his father loved me as one of his own. That's not to say we didn't get along—we really did. I love that man and always will. Vinnie was great with the boys. Whenever we went out drinking and eating after we filmed some TV, Vinnie was there with us as one of the boys. I loved that. The bruddas would all go around and rag on each other. Everyone always picked on me, because I was so quiet. I am still a very sensitive and shy guy. Sometimes I don't want to be in a crowd, because I don't always understand what people are talking about. They use words I don't understand, and sometimes I have to ask, "What does that mean?"

> "Jimmy was a little more restless. I could tell it was something more than the alcohol. His personality didn't change, but he was just not quite on the ball or quite as sharp. He was still good old Jimmy, but he was edgier and a little more paranoid about what was going on around him. He was more conscious of who was looking at him and the things that were said about him."
> —*Gerald Brisco*

Back in the day, Vinnie would cut loose with us. He was not like a boss watching over us. He was good to us all. But Vince Sr. imagined me on top, and then it became clear—first with Bob Backlund, and shortly after that with Hulk Hogan—that I was not going to be winning the belt. I remember right after *Rocky III*, Vinnie wanted Hogan to be the top star.

I still get along with Hogan and respect the brudda for everything that he has done, but he rubbed me the wrong way at first. Early on, when he was trying to make a name for himself, we were wrestling a show in Los Angeles, and he got pissed at me. We were a tag team facing Cowboy Bob Orton and Don Muraco. As you know, Don and I had been wrestling each other for years, so we knew how to get heat. While Hogan was posing in the ring, we were popping the crowd, just as we had been doing for years. Hogan was stunned. You could see it in his face. Don and I just went at it and left Bob and Hulk in the ring together. The gimmick was we continued our fight in the locker room.

After the match, I remember Hogan came into the locker room pissed off. He charged in and said he didn't want me to take on Bob Orton anymore. I guess he didn't want me to get over in any of his matches. I just remember saying to him, "Are you talking to this piece of ass? Are you talking to this piece of ass?" I was so insulted by what he said my eyes were bulging out of my head. He eventually walked away, and that was it. We got along after that, but I know that might've screwed me. As the months went by, I felt as if I was being buried.

THAT PIPER'S PIT AND LEAVING IT ALL BEHIND

One feud I loved was the one against my friend Roddy Piper. The fans loved it, too. You'll notice I say I love everybody in this book, but it's true. I can get along with anybody. I just let everything go and hold no grudges. I remember Tito Santana once told everybody that he was the top babyface, and that I was number two. People would tell me what he thought, and I was like, "Okay, well, God bless him." If he thought he was number one, that's fine. Same thing with Hogan…we were fine after that first run-in. Things went the same way with Piper and me, too.

Roddy Piper and I had a great storyline. We spent hours planning our famous edition of Piper's Pit—you know the one, where he brought in all the bananas, pineapples, and coconuts to make me feel like I was back on the island. When we were rehearsing that, I told Piper to hit me with the coconut. He looked at me like I was crazy, but I knew it'd heat the crowd up. He asked me if I was sure, and I was like, "Brudda, you better hit me with that…"

Roddy did just that, and things went nuts from there. I loved it. The two of us were like oil and water on TV. I remember Piper had so much heat on him—it was like nothing we had ever seen before. Piper's Pit was just completely unbelievable. I feuded with Piper for a while, but I feel we never got to finish the story because I ended up leaving the WWF.

"I was a huge Rowdy Roddy Piper fan as a lad, so much so that I wore a kilt to all the local arenas: Madison Square Garden, Nassau Coliseum, Mrs. Sclafani's ninth-grade English class. Needless to say I had an unhealthy infatuation with the rowdy Scot. So, it would make sense that the Saturday morning in the summer of 1984 when Roddy smashed Jimmy Snuka in the head with a coconut quickly became the greatest day of my misdirected life. I believed every bit of it. All my friends said the coconut was pre-cut—thus the clean break into dozens of pieces. They said there's no way a man can break a coconut over another human man's head. I thought in most cases this was true, but because it was Roddy swinging the mighty fruit, there was a chance.

"So, we and I'm sure hundreds of other perplexed teens purchased coconuts that week. I'm guessing coconut sales went up that summer somewhere in the neighborhood of 3,000 percent, similar to what happened to library cards when Fonzie applied for one. Anyway, one after the other we took turns smashing coconuts against each other's heads, and not one broke. Years later I had the privilege of telling Roddy Piper this story, and he swears on his kids the Snuka coconut was not manipulated. And you know what? I believe him. Of course, I've been concussed for nearly 30 years, so take it for what it's worth. Either way—God bless Jimmy Snuka and his comically dense skull."
—Sal Iacono, "Cousin Sal" on Jimmy Kimmel Live!

I had some good storylines with Piper, and also had some good tag matches and setups with Hogan against Bob Orton and Roddy, but I was not given the status I deserved. I just felt Vinnie gave Hogan the push I deserved. When I was cut out of the first WrestleMania and he brought in Mr. T in what should've been my place, it was a slap in the face. God bless Mr. T, he's a good brudda, but he didn't know anything about wrestling. I just felt like it was payback, and started wondering what was going on. I should've been in the main event *wrestling*—not just in a corner with Hogan. I kept working for a bit after that, but I realized it was time for me to quit WWF. I remember taking Sharon with me to meet with Vinnie, and I came up to him and said, "I'd like to sit down and talk with you, brudda." I told him I wanted to thank him and his family for the opportunities I had. I told him his father was an honest man and a very good businessman, and the only reason I was there to talk to him was to tell him, "I'm done." I remember telling him I didn't owe them anything, and they didn't owe me anything, and that I wanted to be let out of my contract. I remember him crying and begging me to stay. But it was over. I told him I needed to leave, and that was it.

I stuck around and had a few more matches—I think I teamed with my good friend and fellow pro Ricky "The Dragon" Steamboat a bit—but I was pretty much done after WrestleMania.

> **"The thing you have to remember is, when he first hit it big in the WWF, he was already close to 40. He could still go, but it wasn't like he was 27. He spent his prime years in Portland, and there was nothing wrong with that."**
> —Dave Meltzer

Look, I've had a bunch of bangups here or there, but I never had terrible injuries that made me think I was finished or close to it. I have no plans to say good-bye. I also never thought age would hold me back, brudda. I was always ready to go. I left the WWF because I felt I wasn't being used right. I admit I wasn't an easy

brother to deal with. No matter why I left, I can honestly say that I feel bad that I let my fans down, but I just had to leave. I remember returning to Hawaii and seeing myself in a cartoon called *Hulk Hogan's Rock 'n' Wrestling*. That was cool to be a cartoon, brudda. My kids loved it. I loved it, but there was no question it was weird. The cartoon was on the air after I had already left Vinnie.

"Everybody who knew Jimmy during his peak days had a ton of respect for the man. I think Jimmy was kind of at the end of his run. We all have our peak years and then have a downslide. When he got on drugs, he was already on the downslide, and it induced him to get rolling on that stuff. It was his shoulder, neck, and everything else catching up with him, and drugs were a crutch. I don't think it had any effect on his ability. His ability was already waning because of injuries."

—*Gerald Brisco*

For years, Vinnie tried to replace me, but no one could take over for the Superfly. Siva Afi was a good friend of mine. We were tag team partners before I left WWF. I guess they asked him to do the Superfly gimmick—he called himself Superfly Afi. I heard about it when I came back from a trip overseas. Vince came to me and apologized for using Siva Afi. I could have sued him for that, but I didn't because he knew what he did. That was the end of that. I was not mad at Siva. It was not his fault. He needed to make money, too. It's just business. I knew I could never be replaced, and they still have not found anyone who can replace me. As my old friend Lou Albano would say, "You can often imitate me but you cannot duplicate me," or something like that, brudda!

CHAPTER 4

HOMEWARD BOUND

"Sometimes Jimmy and I got a room with double beds.
We would go to sleep, and I would wake up with Jimmy sitting
on my bed having a conversation with someone, and there
were only the two of us in the room. I asked him who he
was talking to, and he said, 'It doesn't make no difference.'"
—Rocky Johnson

After I quit the WWF, I started to realize that maybe the drugs weren't making me feel better after all. I quit the company on my terms, but the downtime really made me give drugs some second thoughts. I decided to go to back to Hawaii, and just like usual, I was able to find peace once I was back in my natural habitat, brudda. The islands were my rehab. I finally said, "Brudda, that's it," and I quit cocaine and steroids. My body felt weak for a little while, but I eventually worked my way through it all.

I was able to appreciate life again by just appreciating the beauty of Hawaii. I love that place so much. It's a place where I feel at home. One house I owned was on Laie Point, and I wish now that I had never sold it. When I go back to Hawaii, I always stop to see how the place is doing. It is a beautiful spot. People on the island still call it "Snuka's house." I wish it still was, brudda. I miss that place.

> "One of my favorite stories of Pops' is that we always had the best dogs. My favorite dog was our white German shepherd, Fresca. I think Pops got her as a puppy from The Iron Sheik, but I can't be certain. One of my other fond memories is of playing in the yard when Pops would be out tending to the yard. We had such a beautifully landscaped lawn because of him."
> —Ata Snuka Campbell, Jimmy's daughter

I am very sad now when I hear that a young guy passed away because of drugs. I always wish I could have helped them somehow. I guess nobody talked to them, or maybe they just didn't listen. I always talk to the guys in the locker room and tell them to take care of themselves. I didn't take care of myself, but I learned from my mistakes. I am not an educated man, and I had to learn the hard way. Today, everyone knows how bad drugs are for you. Some of the boys just want to make it big so badly, they're willing to do anything it takes to get to the top. But it catches up with you, brudda. It's so sad. It's not just wrestling, either— young kids playing sports are taking drugs to give themselves muscles, and they don't want to listen. When you're young, you don't think anything can hurt you. I know I felt that way back in the day. I've told you I was a rascal, and I know I thought nothing could stop me. But I've learned my lessons, brudda.

MEETING MY REAL FATHER IN NEW ZEALAND

I took time out from wrestling to meet my real father when I was around 40. (By then, I had already met his biological daughter and my stepsister, Ada Rose.) As I wrote earlier, I saw him at the pier with Henry while leaving for the Gilbert Islands, but I didn't know he was my dad until I was a teenager. When I found out that Ben Thomas was living in New Zealand, I really wanted to meet him right away. My auntie—my mother's older sister— still spoke with him, so I was able to track him down. I wanted to meet him for a long time, brudda. I wanted to know what his deal was—who he was, and what made him tick. I ended up staying with him for a few days, and it really was amazing. His family has always been so welcoming to me and my family. They also shared great stories about my father, and filled the holes I needed to know about who he was as a man and his background.

I remember walking to his house after arriving in New Zealand and wondering what he'd look like. He knew what I had become, but I still wanted to impress him, so I came with two bottles of Crown Royal. As I got closer to the door, my heart was racing. When the door opened, I looked him up and down, and I said, "Oh my God!" I looked just like him. He may have been "half-cast" like me, but he looked really Fijian. He was something else, brudda. He was this big old man—he stood about 6'6". When he opened that door, he said, "Come on in, son," as if he had known me his whole life.

We drank and talked for hours. My old man could drink, brah! And he talked a lot. He told me about where he came from, and after we met his family, he told me more about his life. I learned that my father's father, who was also named Charles

Wimbledon Benjamin, was an engineer by trade. He was sent to Fiji by Queen Victoria to build the first big bridge and to build the main roadways. While he was doing that, he met my father's mother. She was an *Adi*—which meant a princess in Fijian—of a village called Viseisei, Vuda. When my father was born, he said his parents wanted to take him to Lautoka to be raised, but the elders of the village asked that he stay, because of his royal status or something like that.

Several years later, a heavy machine operator named Mr. Ahtach was working on a road project, and he fell in love with my grandmother. He ended up taking her away to Ovalau, and my father went with them. Mr. Ahtach adopted him eventually. So, my father had been using Ahtach as his last name for quite some time. He would change his name to his father's last name later in life, just before he moved to New Zealand. Back then, the way I understand it, it was easier to get in that country if you had an English-sounding last name. By comparison, the name Wimbledon, my father's family told me, was a very wealthy-sounding name. It was a sign you were well off. I do remember being told at one point that my father's family may have founded the first sugar refinery in Fiji. My father also told me how much he loved Fiji. After his first marriage, he got remarried there to a woman named Tina. The two of them never had children of their own, but they each had some from past marriages.

Anyway, after talking and sharing memories, my father and I said our good-byes. I hoped it would be the start of a new relationship, and he asked me to come back with my kids and grandkids. Sadly, he died shortly after I left. I wish I had gotten to know him better, but I'm so thankful I had those few days in New Zealand. He was an impressive man, and I've carried his picture in my wallet ever since the day I left his house. The picture is a reminder of who this man was, and what life might have been like had I always had my real father in my life. What kind of man might I have become had I not been beaten and raised by Bernie Reiher? It makes me think, but like I always say, you cannot change the past. You must live in the present. I will always remember the short time I had with my real father, and I feel blessed to have known him.

ILY: WRESTLING AND RELAXATION IN HAWAII

When I left the WWF and returned to Hawaii, it wasn't like I stopped wrestling altogether. You can't keep the Superfly away from the ring, brudda! Rocky Johnson and I formed our own little company in Hawaii with our wives, Sharon and Ata. Sharon and Ata are both Samoan, and once considered themselves to be sisters. We were all tight for a long time. I consider Rocky to be my brother, and Ata my sister. I think of their son, Dwayne "The Rock" Johnson, as a nephew. It's always been that way. Our kids grew up with each other. Jimmy Jr. and Dwayne are around the same age, and they have stayed in touch. All of my children consider Dwayne to be their cousin. We were all tight, and we remain so. We are all family, and I mean that, brudda. They mean the world to me, and I love them all.

> "As a child [Dwayne] was influenced by Jimmy diving off the top ropes. He loved to watch Jimmy and I wrestle, because we had two different styles, and he would go home and try to imitate Jimmy and me."
> —Rocky Johnson

"When I first met Sharon, our bond was instant and natural. We had much in common. Both of us married pro wrestlers. Both of us were well adjusted to keeping kids and the home front healthy, and comfortable while our husbands were on the road working. There was perhaps a handful of Samoans in wrestling at the time. Over the years, along with our growing kids, we all became very close as families. Little did we know that one day our boys and one girl would grow up and morph into The Rock, Deuce, and Tamina. How cool is that?"
—*Ata Maivia Johnson*

Dwayne was like one of my kids. The Johnsons would sleep at our home, and the kids would swim together in the pool, or they would play in the gym and I would show them how to lift. My daughters would work out in the gym with me, too. Dwayne was a sweetheart of a kid, so humble, and he always listened to his parents. Rocky and I liked to play cribbage, and our wives would cook and talk. We all had a great time. I knew Dwayne would accomplish whatever he set his mind on. He was good at football, wrestling, and now acting in the movies. He has a special gift and can connect with people on a special level. They can feel his love. You should have seen him dance! The kids would put on shows for us, and Dwayne knew all the island dances. This is what the island people love to do: eat, sing, play the ukulele, dance, and be happy. That is what it's like when I'm home, but on the road it's different.

Hawaii Pro Wrestling didn't run long, but we wished it had. I just didn't work out the way we hoped. We were family and we wanted to work together and take wrestling to a whole new level, especially in Hawaii. But it was just too tough to get the

whole thing off the ground. There were licenses we needed to get, and we had to depend on wrestlers coming back or going to Japan to perform at our events. We also had to compete with Ata's mother's company, which was very hard. It was a lot of work for very little money.

"We started it because originally Jimmy and I were with my father-in-law Peter Maivia's Polynesian Pro Wrestling, and after Peter died, [his wife] Lia took over. She hired Lars Anderson as the booker. At that time, Ata and I owned 49 percent. Lars started bringing in guys that were his friends and they weren't drawing. Neither Jimmy nor I could work with him. In my opinion, he had no idea what he was doing. So, we left and formed our own company."
—Rocky Johnson

I do remember we had one great event, though. A lot of fans showed up to see the show and we made some money off it. The four of us went out for dinner to celebrate. Ata Johnson had the money from the night in a bag next to her seat. After we left, Ata realized she had left the bag at the restaurant. We hurried back, but the money was gone by the time we came back. Like I said, the company just wasn't meant to be. I wish it had worked under different circumstances. It didn't hurt our friendship any. I still love my brother Rocky and sister Ata, that's for sure.

I have so many wonderful memories of spending time with the Johnson family. Rocky and I are brothers, and we are still very close. I might not talk to Rocky for months, and then we'll see each other and just pick up where we left off. It's like no time has passed whenever we get together. Rocky likes to talk, and I am usually quiet. Back in the day, we would drive to a show and he would talk the entire trip, chewing his Red Man tobacco. He would talk so fast that it would just sound like a mumble. I would have to ask him what he was saying, and I have enough trouble understanding people when they're talking slowly!

I had split my time between Hawaii and Japan after I left the WWF, and then Verne Gagne asked me to come back to AWA. Verne and I always got along, and this gave me another opportunity to wrestle with Col. DeBeers and my friend, Bruiser Brody.

I remember getting a call from Lou Albano and Vinnie asking me to come back to the WWF. I think I was in Hawaii at the time, and I was ready. I was not on cocaine anymore—I hadn't been for years—and I started to realize that maybe some of the bad stuff in the WWF was partly my fault. I had missed shows, and they couldn't count on me at all. I messed up.

"It's very easy to slip into a dependency to get up, sleep,
or deal with pain. It's not like football players, who get
seasons to recover. You either work and make money,
or you don't work and make no money. Jimmy's a pretty
tough character. I don't know if he was ever addicted to drugs
or if he just did it. He's one of those guys who has the focus
to stop on his own. If he wants to quit smoking, he can.
He doesn't need one crutch to replace another."
—*Jeff Miller*

Wrestling is a "never say never" business. I've heard that a million times during my career, and so have the fans. So, it probably did not surprise some people in TV wonderland when I returned to Vinnie and the WWF in 1989. This time, I thought, things would be different. Vinnie called me up and told me I'd be in main event matches if I left AWA and came back to the company. He told me he wanted to take me places I had never been before. The money was good, and the timing seemed right, and to be honest, I missed it, brudda. So, I agreed to come back. I was excited. I changed up my look a little bit—putting on boots, for example.

Sadly, it turned out to be the same deal again in the WWF, brah. I wasn't being used right. The things Vinnie had promised me didn't happen yet again. I was mad about that. I need to say this again: Vinnie was like a brother to me. I love him to this day. Like any brothers, though, there are things we fight about. I feel Vinnie was still jealous of me, so he didn't want me to steal the spotlight. I think he brought me back to keep me down. I could be wrong, and I realize that, but it's just the way I feel.

I do think Vinnie was going to give me a chance at Hogan's title, but it never happened. I remember him coming to me and asking me if I'd like to turn heel and wrestle Hogan at WrestleMania. I told him I'd really love to, and I gave him that intense look I used to give my opponents. I was excited about it, but later that day, Vinnie came back to me stone-faced and said he'd changed his mind. He told me Hogan said he didn't want to wrestle "that crazy man." Since Hogan was the company's bread and butter— he was the biggest star the wrestling world had ever seen—the match never happened. For three years, I was used to just help younger guys get over with the fans. I never mind helping out the boys, but I was hoping for more with my comeback, and I felt all these losses were hurting me.

To this day, I've never won a WrestleMania match, and that stings a little. I lost to "Mr. Perfect" Curt Hennig and Ravishing Rick Rude in WrestleManias V and VI, and was the first opponent The Undertaker ever beat, at WrestleMania VII. Henning and Rude were good workers. They became big stars in the business, but the bottom line is the Superfly was losing all the time. I want to say it again—I never minded putting my opponents over. It's part of the business, and I have a deep respect for that tradition. I am honored that The Undertaker started his WrestleMania streak with me. His streak is still going, which is cool. Good for him. He is a very good worker. He has worked hard his whole life, and he deserves to have an unbeaten streak in WrestleMania. His matches are always high-quality, brudda.

While I lost all of those matches, I was getting paid good money, so I never said anything. Just like I did during my first run in the WWF, I kept hanging around in the hopes I'd get my title match. But the opportunity never came, and I left the company again. I did have some good matches with many wrestlers I respected, like Greg "The Hammer" Valentine and The Honky Tonk Man, but I was never elevated to the status I felt I deserved.

I was being used in the midcards instead of main-eventing. I did, however, love tagging with Piper at Survivor Series during that run. I thought that added a new angle to our long-running story.

This time, I think the office had no problem with me leaving. I was not happy, and they weren't happy with the Superfly, I'm sure. Don't get me wrong, I loved being back, but it wasn't going anywhere. I loved the people there, but it was just time to go, and by then, I think Vinnie knew it, too. He just wanted to bury me again. He wanted to keep me out of the main events. I still love him, no matter what, but my feelings are my feelings. Sometimes I wonder if my career would be different if I had joined the WWF when Vince Sr. was still running the show. I wonder if it would have been me headlining WrestleMania. I wonder if I would have gotten as big a push as guys like Hulk Hogan. I wonder about it, but I don't dwell on it. Life is life, and that is that. You cannot live your life in the past. You always have to look forward. But seriously, brudda...I wonder about it all.

> "Jimmy was over like a million dollars. There was no doubt about it—as much so as Hogan was over, without the international push Hogan got. I do believe the drugs were his downfall. He was his own worst enemy. I believe Vince had tried and tried and got tired with him. He was unreliable. Knowing Jimmy now, I think he realizes what drugs did to him."
> —Tito Santana

My career may always be defined by that moment I jumped off the steel cage at Madison Square Garden in New York City, and I'm okay with that, but I have so many other great memories. Thinking back to that match, I know I have another moment like that in me. If my ankle wasn't a problem, I'd be in the ring today, brudda. If I was booked now, I'd be at the arena getting prepared for my match. I love the people out there who appreciate what I do. Being there in the ring, in front of the fans, is everything to me.

I always say this, and I mean it: every match I've ever worked is my favorite. Every opponent is my favorite opponent. Every moment is my favorite moment. My favorite match is the one I'm wrestling at that present time. I just love them all. I know I could come back today and be on my game. I could take on the kids in the business today and show them how it's done. I'd love to teach them all. I would like to teach John Cena a little ring psychology. He's a good brudda, and I know his father. I splashed John's dad at a show we worked together. He asked me if I could do the move on him, and I told him, "I'd do anything for you, brudda." I did it, and I bet he didn't even feel it. I wonder if John's dad told him about it.

I enjoy watching many of today's stars. I still watch wrestling every week. I was just watching the Usos tag team on WWE, and when they came in the ring, they did this Samoan war dance. They wore traditional Fijian *sulus*, and I tell you brudda, it reminded me of what I did way back when. They had a very good tag team match, and I think their timing and psychology are very good—they are throwbacks to the old school. I also like watching Santino Marella, Mick Foley, my nephew Dwayne "The Rock" Johnson, and my daughter Tamina. Rey Mysterio Jr. is one great high-flyer I also have to mention. That brudda can get around the ring!

I'm a fan of wrestling and always will be. I'm so proud of everything I have done in the ring, but I appreciate what others have brought to the business as well. It wasn't always easy to watch the other matches when I was on a card. I was usually backstage, so I often didn't get to see a lot of them. As time has gone on and I find myself at home more, I watch them all on TV. It's hard to single out all the amazing matches I've seen in my life. Brudda, I still remember that cage match Mick Foley had against The Undertaker when Mick was wrestling as Mankind. The Hell in a Cell match the two had, when Mick was thrown off the top of the cage, was amazing. The two of them just went at each other and did things that had never been done before. It was breathtaking, brudda. That's what makes wrestling such amazing entertainment. You remember moments like that one forever. Mick Foley is as fearless as the Superfly. He has done things in the ring I never thought were possible. I also remember the cage match Mick had with Triple H that saw the cage break. The two of them are at the very top in the business. They know how to work together like pros, and how to get the best reaction from the fans.

There are so many other classic matches that I have watched and enjoyed over the years. Junkyard Dog working against the great Terry Funk was a feud I thought was just lovely. Funk is just so good at what he does, and Junkyard Dog told a great story in the ring. I miss that brudda. I also liked watching matches with guys I had a long history with. Don Muraco was so good at making fans go crazy against him. The "magnificent" one and my other brudda, Rowdy Roddy Piper, had a great meeting of the minds when Don wore a kilt in their match. Those two just went at it. There are so many more I could name—like when Bret Hart took on his brother Owen, and the many matches Ric Flair and Ricky Steamboat had, but I choose to just say this: I love everything about wrestling, but what I love most are the matches that aren't just a few minutes of kicking and punching and fighting for no reason. I like the matches that get the fans interested and keep them on the edges of their seats, brudda! Bob Backlund did that when he was in the ring. He took his time and told some great stories. I remember him working against Harley Race, and those two just amazed me. I know Harley Race taught Backlund everything he knew, and those guys were just a pleasure to watch.

Those matches are in the past, but I still get excited to watch wrestling now and possibly see the next classic match. I'm so proud of everything I've done, but I've got to look forward, brah. I have to keep moving. I've had an amazing but difficult life. I take pleasure in the small things as much as I do the big things. You can't let life pass you by. I've made my share of mistakes and have had my highs, but I know that every moment is a gift, brudda.

I had mixed emotions when I was inducted into the WWE Hall of Fame in 1996. Don't get me wrong, brudda. I loved it! I appreciated it. It meant a lot to me. But I was confused a little. I made sure to say during my speech that I wasn't retired. I remember when they were showing the clips of my work, they played the splash off the cage against Don Muraco at Madison Square Garden. I looked over at Vince and I said, "Brudda, that can happen again!" He just looked at me and smiled. It touched me that I got inducted by Don. It was awesome. Not too many guys get in the Hall of Fame. I was happy about that. In my mind, I thought everything that happened before with Vinnie was water under the bridge. I thanked him at the ceremony, and today I carry the ring they gave me everywhere I go.

The fans are the best part of this business, and when I see them on the road, I show them my Hall of Fame ring and say that Vince McMahon did not give this ring to me. I tell them, "All of you beautiful fans gave me this ring." Where would I be

without my fans? If you do not have the fans behind you, you are out of the business. It's that simple. I see fans everywhere I go. I see them in restaurants, parking lots, shopping malls, casinos…I could go on and on. I even see them when I am at the doctor's office. I remember getting an X-ray one time and there was another guy in the waiting room. I knew he recognized me, and I could see him trying to get his wife's attention. I waited for him to come out to the parking lot, and I went up to the car to say hello to him and give him a hug. I learned he had a brain tumor and was no longer able to speak. He was in bad shape. I gave his wife my phone number in case there was anything I could do for them.

A year or so later, I got a call from his brother to tell me he only had a few days left to live, so I went to see him. He knew I was there, and I hung the necklace I was wearing on his hospital bed where he could see it, and then I said good-bye. He died a day or so later, and I really felt the loss, brudda. It is hard to see someone so young pass like that. I have visited many sick people in the hospital, and I know that someday I will also be like them. Hopefully, someone treats me as nicely as I have tried to treat them. Sometimes fans who are in wheelchairs want to visit me, but I say, "No, I will come to you." I went to Walter Reed Hospital and it broke my heart—so many young men and women without arms and legs, all because they were willing to fight for me, for us. I give them the biggest hugs. What else can I do for them? I give them an autograph, and hopefully it makes them happy for a few minutes.

CHAPTER 5

GAINING MY INDEPENDENCE

"I had the opportunity to meet and work with Jimmy on multiple independent events and during the initial years of ECW in Philadelphia. I got to know Jimmy well, and what I most remember about him are his kind and gentle characteristics. He would keep to himself and never cause any problems with anyone. He just did what was asked of him. However, the one thing I noticed about Jimmy was that when he would walk to the ring, a light bulb would go off, and the guy that was sitting backstage would convert into a completely different person. Jimmy Snuka would become the Superfly! Very few wrestlers could hit the switch and become their persona in mere seconds. The ones that stand out to me are Terry Funk, Mick Foley, Sabu, and Jimmy Snuka. Jimmy had the 'it' factor that made him the legend that he is."
—Andy Vineberg, ECW backstage worker

The movie *The Wrestler*, which was originally going to be based on my life (producers called me, but then vanished), showed people how hard the road can be for wrestlers. Some of my brothers are fighting with medical bills after fighting for all those years in the ring. In the movie, Mickey Rourke played a struggling wrestler who is sort of washed up. That's not the Superfly, brudda. Some years are better than others moneywise, but I've done okay.

Since I left the WWF for good, I've worked the independent circuit. It's not an easy life, brudda. You're constantly without a steady paycheck, and you have to go out and find your own bookings. But I've made it work, even to this very day. Sharon booked me early on after I left the WWF, and she screwed me. She was so mean-spirited. I had known that back in the day when she had messed up my travel plans. I admit I no-showed some events, but sometimes it was not my fault. Sharon worked at an airline and would purposely book me on standby, instead of getting me a real seat on a plane. Many times, I'd be stuck at the airport with no way to get to an event because she screwed me over. I'm not saying that was the only reason I no-showed matches, but it was one of them. After the WWF, she did it again, brudda. She would book me for two shows, send me off somewhere, and then pocket the cash from a show I knew nothing about. Since I was paid upfront and she handled all my affairs, she just raked in all of my money, and she almost destroyed my name.

Jeff Miller, who wrestled as Metal Maniac and was a fellow brudda from Hawaii, booked me from about 1990 to 1998, and we made each other some money. Jeff took care of me and made sure I got some good bookings. I also made sure he was booked on each of my shows, because I wanted to help him out, too. After leaving the WWF in February of 1992, I toured Japan again and did a few stints with Eastern Championship Wrestling. I didn't wrestle a lot there—my job was mainly to help build up the organization. Tod Gordon was the promoter back then, and he was a good brudda. He had a lot of respect for me, Don Muraco, and Terry Funk. He knew how much we meant to the business, and he let us show the new guys how it was done.

"Jimmy was the king. He was scary. I remember being in the
locker room to say hello, and my hands were shaking, my
heart was pounding. I was completely starstruck."
—*Jeff Miller*

I became ECW's first heavyweight champion and hit the road
with them through 1994. ECW was a nice payday and I had fun
there. They didn't do shows often—just once a month or something, I think. The belt was nice to have, but I was never a glory
guy. It was a good time, but I have a good time no matter where
I go. I really loved getting back in the ring with Don Muraco
in ECW. The two of us were still magic together. We probably
would still have it if we got back in the ring today, brudda!

ECW was a good gig, but things changed for the Superfly
when Paul Heyman took over. Paul was a smart booker and
had been around the wrestling business for a long time, but I
didn't really like working with him. He changed the name to
Extreme Championship Wrestling, and he rubbed me the wrong
way from the start. I didn't know Tod was leaving, or that Paul
was going to buy the company from him. I just remember all of
a sudden, Paul came to me and said, "Hey, I want you to wrestle Terry Funk and I want you to put him over." I handed the
belt to him, and said, "Brudda, here's the belt." I didn't have a
problem with losing the belt. It's only a gimmick. I was not mad
at him, but I quickly found out what kind of guy he was. He
came in, and he was different. He went about business differently. He bought the company, and right away he had his own
crew. I didn't stay there long, because I just felt out of place. I
know Paul Heyman did great things and brought in a new era of
"extreme" wrestling, but I just didn't feel like I could be part of

that, brudda. I was old school—more on building a match and telling a story without going for chair shots and stuff like that. Plus, even though I never cared much about winning a title, I was pretty pissed off that I had to drop that title right off the bat just because Heyman asked me to.

In the end, all that mattered to me was that the fans were happy they spent their money on a ticket and that I put on the best match possible. That was true in ECW too, brudda. One match I had against Tommy Dreamer was big, because it was the first time anyone kicked out of my splash. Paul Heyman had asked me if Tommy Dreamer could do it, because it would make for good television. I didn't care about that. I thought it was cool because it had never been done before. I thought it was good for business, so I said, "Why not?" Again, I'm not a glory guy, so we did it.

> "It was a simple, easy match, but I remember the finisher just like it was yesterday. For me to kick out of that sacred finisher, it was unheard of. When I kicked out, the place went silent. The crowd was shocked. Then he looked at me with those crazy Jimmy eyes, yelled at me that 'I fucked up,' and hit me four more times. He still beat me, but it was shock value. That stuff was never done before. It was one of the first stepping stones in my career. Paul had known Jimmy, and Jimmy was cool with it, and he was well compensated for it."
> —Tommy Dreamer

GOOD-BYE TO ECW

Since 1994, I've been on my own. I've been lucky to be able to continue wrestling and have a career in the ring, but independents are a lot of work. You don't have a big company doing every-thing for you. Whether it was me or Jeff, we would have to get ourselves booked on a show, rather than having an organization arrange all that and give us a steady paycheck. Again, it was not hard for me to get work, but it took more energy. I don't feel like the character in *The Wrestler*. He was a guy who was lonely and lost his family. I just want to keep performing. It's true the road can be hard; you don't have time to heal yourself and you miss your family. But if you love the business and love being in the ring, then it doesn't matter if there are 50 people in the arena or 500. I just give the fans everything I've got, brudda.

> **"Jimmy was such an in-ring performer. It didn't matter, and I really mean this, if Jimmy was at Madison Square Garden or a small crowd in Texas. If he was in the ring, it didn't matter. He performed to his very best, and he did it night after night."**
> —*Terry Funk*

It's true that the money isn't always good on the circuit, but you don't have a choice. The promoters are also hard sometimes. You have a lot of little guys trying to be big guys. They are hop-ing to make enough money on the show to pay you. I haven't been stiffed in pay much, but I'm sure I've been taken advantage of. I've worked shows where a promoter will run out the back after a match and not pay you, but I would go straight to their place and ask for the money. I'd just tell them, "I am here to see my money." When they saw the look in my eyes, I would just tell them, "Brudda, you're very lucky I love you."

"There were times promoters tried to get over on me and Jimmy but weren't able to. People were scared to death of Jimmy. I mean, look at him. One day, Jimmy came in to do an interview with ECW. He was there with Don [Muraco], and [Paul] Heyman is directing, and everyone is standing around watching Jimmy. The first thing Heyman says is, 'Oh my God, you look like you go into the Olympia.' He just looked so freaky. Promoters tried to play with me, and if it got out of hand, all I needed to do was put Jimmy on the phone. Most times that didn't happen."
—Jeff Miller

To this day, I need to work. The royalties I receive from the WWE are nice, but some years are better than others. I've been lucky in that Vinnie asks me to do guest spots every so often. It's not a lot of money each time out, but being on TV helps me get more money on the independents, and it reminds promoters that I am still a big draw. It also lets my fans know that I'm still out there. I love it, and I'll always keep coming back when asked. It means the world to me to be with all you lovely people and to see you react to what I do in the ring.

In 2007, I wrestled Chris Jericho with Rowdy Roddy Piper, Mickey Rourke, and Ricky "The Dragon" Steamboat at WrestleMania XXV, and it was so great to be on the biggest stage in the world. It was also sweet because it was the 25th anniversary of WrestleMania. Our feud started off as kind of a reenactment of Piper's Pit, in that I would fall on the set and Chris would continue to beat me with boards and stuff like that. I remember telling Jericho, who is a good brudda, that if he was going to hit me with those boards, he better make it look good. Brudda, did he ever! I was black and blue! Jericho is one of the best in

the business. He's so good at the mic and with promos, and he trained with Stu Hart in Canada and knows the business inside and out. The first time I met Stu Hart, he was already in a wheelchair. I never wrestled for him or with him. I did work with his son Bret Hart, and he was a very talented wrestler. I never got to wrestle Owen Hart, but I could see he was also good inside the ring. Stu was a good teacher. He was very old school—he would stretch those bruddas! He would either make you or break you.

Jericho and I had a good time in the ring. That WrestleMania match was great because we had old school and new school. It's about business, and not about egos. Sure, I would like to win all the time, but that is not going to happen. You have to help the younger guys, and it's good for the business. Everyone gets a turn, and it's now the younger guys' turn. Like I said, Chris is a good wrestler, and I loved being in the ring again with Ricky, Piper, and Ric Flair, who was in our corner. Mickey Rourke also turned out to be a good guy, and he did a very good job in *The Wrestler*.

Altogether, that match was a decent payday and I had a good year financially, but I think I should've made more for being in a WrestleMania match. How many other guys over 60 years old could be in WrestleMania, brudda?

As for the independent circuit, it's important that you all know there are so many good wrestlers in the indies who just need a lucky break. Sal Sincere gives 100 percent and uses psychology and knows his way around a ring. Other guys who stand out for me are The Merengue Warrior and Andrew "The Reinforcer" Anderson. In the wrestling world, I respect everybody. If they work hard, it doesn't matter to me if they are WWE superstars or wrestling at a local gym. I give them my respect and love them all, brudda.

THE TRUTH ABOUT SHARON, MY MARRIAGE, AND MY MONEY

Sharon and I divorced in 1997, but it was over a long time before that. I loved her at one time, but she and I were like oil and water most of the time. We just didn't mix well. After a while, everything must come to an end. I was monkeying around all the time, and I know she was, too. I also know she loved the lifestyle I provided for her, and that got under my skin. She couldn't get enough of my money, brudda. The best thing that Sharon gave me were my four children: Jimmy, Liana, Sarona, and Ata.

She is the mother of my children, and I will always love her for that. There were good times, no doubt. We always had something going on, teaching the kids our culture and how to dance and sing. We would put on shows in our backyard, and Sharon would play the ukulele and guitar. She also taught the kids how to play. My girls are beautiful singers. We had barbecues almost every weekend at our home in Portland. The neighbors would come and bring food also. It was a good time.

I'll say this, brudda—Sharon was a good cook, and she made sure the kids learned how to cook. But at the barbecues, the men did all the cooking. Little Jimmy and I would cut up all the chicken, steak, *taro* (it's like purple potato), green bananas, rice, and pork. We would start early in the morning and dig a big hole in the backyard. We would then line it with big, hot river rocks, and covered the hot rocks with large banana leaves. Then we'd put the pig in there, cover it with banana leaves and a big piece of canvas, and then cover it with dirt. You don't want any steam to get out of there, brah! You let the pig stay in there for about five hours, and then it's done. The best you ever ate! It broke da mouth, brudda. (That is the Hawaiian pidgin way of saying, "It tastes so good that my mouth is broken and I don't need to eat again!")

> **"Jimmy and Sharon were your usual wrestling couple.**
> **He was out on the road, and whenever he'd come home, she'd**
> **be excited like a little puppy. But sometimes couples don't**
> **make it. I don't think it's totally his fault, but I'm probably biased.**
> **I think she was very happy with the lifestyle he afforded her.**
> **She wanted to go out and do incredible things she wouldn't**
> **have been able to have done on her own. His money paid for**
> **her family to invest in real estate. That family benefited**
> **more than we did—not that we were out for it. Jimmy was**
> **larger than life, and that was just natural for us."**
> —Louise Reiher

It's sad, but Sharon and I didn't treat our marriage the way we should have, and I regret the impact it might have had on our children. I wish I could have been around my children more. My career made it hard for me to always be around, and I regret missing their birthdays, holidays, and other special occasions. But I couldn't help it, brudda. I am so thankful that they allowed me to be away from them to do something I loved. I taught them as much as I could, and I just hope they know how much I love them and always wanted to be with them. Whenever I worked close to home, I would come home after a match, even if it meant getting in at 3:00 AM, just to see them. I would pull in the driveway, which was close to Jimmy's window, and he knew the sound of my car. It would wake him up, and Sharon would get mad because I'd go get him out of his crib, sit him on my lap, and have an early meal. I enjoyed that time with my son. I would chew on my food and then feed it to Jimmy. That is how the "Polys" do it: the mother would sit on the floor with her legs crossed, and then chew the food and put little bits on her legs for the baby to crawl up and eat. After the baby ate, the mother would rub the baby with coconut oil, and then they would fall asleep, brudda. When we lived at the Point in Hawaii, Sharon's mother would come over and massage the kids as they fell asleep.

"We were such a connected family, and nothing could break it. The divorce was very hard on our family, but things happen for a reason, and it was for the best. They are both in a good place now."
—Sarona Snuka-Polamalu

"They didn't fight all the time. That was some of the time. My dad was a very intense person, but loving as well. He'd get on my case if I wasn't doing something right or if I was being disrespectful. But there was a lot of love in our house, even though they fought. We always felt our dad loved us. It was a rough childhood in a lot of different ways, but thank goodness I had a good relationship with my dad. Even though he wasn't home all the time, he was always supportive in whatever we were going to do. Right after they got divorced—that first year—we didn't speak for like a year and a half. I was young-minded and very immature in my thinking. I've grown up a lot. Time has a way of healing stuff. I realized life is too short, and my dad and I should mend things. We've always been very tight."

—*Jimmy Snuka Jr.*

I had all my checks from the WWF sent directly to our home so that Sharon could provide for our family. I took a small draw from all of my shows, but most of it went to her. I can honestly say now that I have none of the money I earned during my biggest days in the WWF. I never saw any of my checks from the WWF. I'd ask Sharon to show me where the money went, but she never did. I remember Liana joked about being my secretary, because she'd answer phones for me and stuff. I asked her where the money was. I know she was on my side. She even hid some checks from Sharon.

I bought my family many beautiful homes, but I loved my home in Hawaii the most. We had homes in Vancouver, Charlotte, Cherry Hill, New Jersey, and Orem, Utah. We had moved to Utah, by the way, because Jimmy Jr. was already going to college there. It seemed like a nice place. I wrestled there with the WWF back in the day, and it was lovely. No matter where we lived, I always provided for my family, brudda. In my opinion, Sharon benefited the most from the money I made with the WWF. I know there were times that she left the children with her sister to go on big trips of her own when I was on the road. She'd also constantly fly in all of her family from Western Samoa to stay in our house. I've heard she and her family invested my money in other properties. I don't know if that's true, but I regret being too trusting of people.

"The incredible truth is that, no matter how hard times got, none of us ever entertained the thought of looking for another way of life. There was a tremendous amount of driving and living on the road in those days. It was okay for the single guys, but for guys with big families, family life suffered. We moved to every territory that Rocky was booked in, whether it was for a year, two years, or six months. It was easy for us, we were just a family of three. Rocky, Dwayne, and I could just pick up and go! But for Sharon and Jimmy, with four growing kids, moving the entire household across country was very difficult. More often than not, the only solution was for him to travel and work, leaving Sharon to uphold the house and raise the kids. Many of the wrestling families made that same decision. That's a hard lifestyle, dealing with the burdens of single parenting, and struggling with a long-distance relationship. No doubt, that puts great strains on a marriage, and quite possibly, proved to be too much to bear."

—Ata Maivia Johnson

I didn't mind being away from Sharon the last years of our marriage. She made life hell for me when we were together. It was hard to always be on the road and to not see my children, and then when I did come home, I'd have to see Sharon, too. I would always look forward to seeing my kids, but toward the end of my marriage with Sharon, I dreaded seeing her. I knew she would push all of my buttons and we would get into a fight. I hate that the kids saw that side of me. I always wanted to make sure that whenever I was home, they would enjoy our time together. I tried my best, brudda, I really did, but Sharon egged me on. We would fight and fight and fight. She pressed all of my buttons. I didn't hit her to hurt her. I just wanted to stop her. Wrestlers know how to hit without hurting the other person.

"Unfortunately, because my parents were divorced when I was 11, I did not have a whole lot of time with Pops. Of what I can recall, though, I know I enjoyed the little time that I had with him. That was one of the negatives. He was on the road a lot for wrestling. I know that he tried to spend as much time as he could when he was home. It was very tough saying good-bye to Pops. It seemed like he was always leaving to go wrestle. The joy is that at least we were able to see him on television. But it was not the same as having him home. It was fun when we got to go on trips. We also loved when he returned from overseas, because he would bring presents from wherever he went.

"Because I was young at the time, I would say the pluses were that my friends thought I had one of the coolest dads. Granted, most of my friends were boys. I believe I was in fourth or fifth grade when he was one of the chaperones for my field trip to an art museum. I remember all the boys in the class, including those who weren't my friends, wanted to be in my group.

"When we got to the museum, it was the chaperone's duty to explain to the kids about each painting—the painter, the name of the artwork, the medium used. Pops would go up to each piece and say, 'Okay bruddas, so dis painting is the kine that was beautiful and da artist is so good.' Or something to that effect. I just remember all the kids were entranced by anything he said. So, it didn't matter if what he said made sense or not. I thought that was such a funny experience."

—Ata Snuka Campbell

We named our youngest daughter Ata, after our dear sister, Ata Johnson. Our Ata was born in 1981, and I knew right away she was not mine. That didn't mean I loved her any less though, brudda. She was a beautiful girl, and I really wanted to raise her as one of our own. That didn't mean I wasn't pissed off, though. I was angry and mad as hell at Sharon. We hadn't really been having sex and Sharon had cheated on me many times, so I knew for sure this kid was not mine. I had seen her affairs with my own eyes, brudda. One time after I got home from the gym, I saw all the lights in the house were off but there was a car in the driveway. When I went upstairs, the bedroom door was locked. I busted in and saw her with a guy who went to the same church we did. She could've been honest with me. She knew I was cheating. We yelled a lot at each other, and I have to be honest, we just went at it. She hit me with frying pans, her hands, and whatever else she could throw at me. I tried not to, but I have to admit, I hit her. It wasn't hard—just enough to stop her. We hit each other, and I feel bad we did it with the kids in the house.

After that fight with Sharon, that was it for us. One day someone came to me and served me divorce papers. I told the process server to shove it up her ass. But the divorce eventually went through. I just wanted out, brudda.

> "I was young at the time but I do remember the fights, and they were loud and physical. As a child, I was very scared to hear them fight and all the bangs against the wall. I do remember hearing my mom hit the wall. I hated hearing the yelling, because

Sharon, me, and our three girls: Ata, Sarona, and Liana

I never knew why it was happening. I think the hardest thing would be that because Pops was away so often, I wanted the time he spent at home to be a happy time. As a child, you never understand all that parents go through. To be honest, I think that the fights were brought on by both parties. I think they both knew how to push one another's buttons. I will never condone physical violence with a husband hitting his wife or vice versa. But then again, I think that both my parents have very short tempers that can be set off easily when built up enough. I do know all that built-up anger can destroy a person.

"My mom knows how to push buttons and say the things that hurt the most. I know Pops wasn't an educated man, and I almost wonder if that fact wasn't used against him by my mother. I almost wonder if the beatings were his way to fight back. I don't know. But it is never right to use physical violence unless you're fighting for your life. I lived with my mom most of my life, so I only got her side of the story. She would always talk about the beatings and that Pops was always drunk or high. I'm sure that happened a lot. He was drunk and high a lot. She said he would make her get high, too. I wouldn't put it past him, but I just don't know. He never hit us kids or anything."
—Ata Snuka Campbell

I love my Ata so much. I love all of my children, and even though Ata is not my biological daughter, I always loved her as one of my own. It is not her fault her mother had an affair.

Ata was involved in a terrible car accident when she was 14. She was in a coma for a month. I remember visiting her, and Sharon didn't want me to be there. Sharon and Sarona were also in the accident, but they weren't hurt as badly. I am so glad Ata came out of the accident okay. I love her dearly.

It was Ata and Liana's decision several years ago to get a DNA test to see who Ata's father was. I honestly didn't ask for a DNA test, but Liana worked in a hospital and had the opportunity to get it done. The test revealed the truth—a truth this brudda already knew, but Ata didn't know for sure until that moment

"It was really hard. Liana and Sarona called me when the results came back. We all cried together. I called my best friend and cried with her. It's just a hard thing to learn, especially since my mom had lied to me. She was angry I did the test, and she got a little physical with me. She said she had told me [the truth], but if she did, why would she be afraid I was doing it? She said she told me before the car accident. My mom is a very headstrong lady. A lot of secrets have been hidden.

"The way I thought about it was I had two stepdads: Pops and Ricky Georgi, my [actual] stepfather. I didn't know my real dad. That's why I did it. I love my siblings. I love Pops. I'm grateful our relationship is back. I will always love him as a dad, just as I love Ricky as a dad."
—Ata Snuka Campbell

I don't speak to Sharon much anymore. I speak with my children, but not as often as I would like. I think Sharon's stories have really hurt my relationship with them. I'm sad about that. I love all of my children and all of my grandchildren. I think all my years of cheating, drinking, and using drugs made Sharon hate me and want to see me suffer. In many ways, she has succeeded. I don't have much money, and I am not as close to my children as I would hope. I will say it again—we rushed into marriage and stayed in it too long.

"As far as my mom goes, I think she has built-up hatred
toward him, and she's taking that out on him. I know that
they loved each other but had a funny way of showing it.
I wouldn't say it was a strong marriage, because of all
the problems, but I think both of them were not ready
for the commitment or time it took to be in such a relationship.
I know they both love all of their kids, but I just think that
we might have been the reason they stayed together. Again,
I don't know this for a fact, it is more just a feeling."
—Ata Snuka Campbell

CHAPTER 6

A NEW LEASE ON LIFE

"I was married for 24 years, and then my husband got a girlfriend who I didn't like as much as he did. So, I was separated, and I wasn't really getting out there again. I have three children of my own. One night, I did someone a favor and went to a restaurant to keep a friend who had just got a job there company. She didn't know anybody. I brought my sister with me, and in [Jimmy] came. He was wearing a two-piece workout outfit with a speckled-striped print, a headband, ponytail, and slippers. I said to my sister, 'Who is that?'"
—Carole Snuka, Jimmy's wife

The early to mid-1990s weren't exactly my best years. I was working independents, and my messy marriage was heading toward divorce. I certainly was not looking for love, that's for sure, but it found the Superfly yet again. It was September of 1993 when I met Carole Maston. I didn't think she'd end up being the love of my life or that she'd save my life when I met her at a local hangout in New Jersey. I know she didn't expect anything either.

I was at this restaurant, and some people came up to me and asked me for autographs. I had just done an independent show, so there were a bunch of people there, and a few of them bought me drinks. There was this one woman there who was really annoying me. She was just in my face, brudda. So, I decided to walk over to Carole. I was just trying to get away from that other woman.

> "He sent us drinks, and he motioned like he was toasting me. I remember thinking, *Is he toasting me?* I looked behind me to see if he was toasting someone else and realized nobody was behind me, so I toasted him back. Then he walked over, and asked me for a favor. He told me, 'This blonde girl is chasing me around, can I just stand here and say I'm with you?' I said, 'Yeah,' not sure that it'd work. After that, we started talking, and then he invited me to his show the next night.
>
> "After the show, he asked me for my phone number. I gave it to him, but I didn't think he'd even remember my name. I was surprised a month later when he called me. I made my sister go out with us again, but eventually I went out with him alone. I just figured I was his girl in Jersey—that he had a girl in Connecticut, and so on. I didn't see any harm in going out for dinner. It was six or nine months before I told anyone I knew that I went out with him."
>
> —Carole Snuka

Carole really straightened me out. After I met her, I thought maybe it was the Lord's way of giving me somebody to help me take care of myself. She turned me into a good boy. I was still drinking and womanizing at the time, and she helped me settle down. She turned into my guardian angel, and helped me get my business in order. We dated for many years, and when I went to Las Vegas to train Jimmy Jr. in 2001, we kept a long-distance relationship going.

"After my kids all met him, then I let him stay. My kids were all grown and out of the house, but I wanted them to meet him first. My son Dennis thought it was really cool. He was a wrestling fan and loved Jimmy as a kid. I remember one time Dennis brought a girl to the house, and Jimmy was in his trunks with a hatchet cutting branches in the yard. The girl was like, 'There's a man outside your house in his underwear.' Dennis was like, 'Oh, that's just the Superfly.'

"My other kids were happy for me, too. My daughter, Bridget, was just happy I was going out. My son Rich was a little skeptical. He wanted to meet him right away. I was so nervous that they wouldn't get along, and then Rich came home from college and ended up talking to Jimmy all night over a couple of beers."
—Carole Snuka

"I definitely did not approve of my mom dating Jimmy when I found out. My opinion was that he would only hurt her, and why was the Superfly interested in my mom? At the time, I was finishing my college career and preparing for the NFL. After a very odd introduction, Jimmy ended up teaching me about money, people, stress, family, friends, and the media. Recently, what I learned most from Jimmy is his patience. Jimmy truly understands that life is about family and friends and nothing else. Jimmy is an amazing man—I have literally seen him give the shirt off of his back to someone. He has been like the big brother that I never had. He's the most caring, patient man I've ever met. I haven't heard Jimmy raise his voice in 17-plus years."
—Rich Maston, Carole's son

GIVING SOMETHING BACK AND TRAINING MY CHILDREN

My whole career I've believed in doing what's best for the fans first and foremost. I just love being in that ring, and it doesn't matter whether I win, lose, or draw—just as long as I'm in there! So, when my son asked me to teach him how to wrestle in 2001, I was excited about it. He had been a cameraman for NBC in Salt Lake City, and he was doing really well with his career. I was already so proud of him for going to college. He was a good, educated young man with a career of his own. Deep down, I thought he would eventually get into the wrestling business. It was just something I always knew. When he decided to break into the business, I remember asking him, "Are you sure?" I wanted to be certain he knew what to expect and to be ready for it. He said he was, so I said, "Okay, let's go." I asked him how badly he wanted it, and he just stared at me. That's when I knew. It was in his bones.

"My dad didn't want to push me into the business. I was a cameraman and working as a youth counselor, but I was kind of playing with the idea. A lot of people were saying I should. One night, I was in a room with four or five of my cousins, and they all said to go wrestle. That is what started the thought process. My auntie Ata, The Rock's mother, was the biggest thing for me. She came to Utah to visit my dad and my sisters, and I was watching The Rock wrestle. I talked to Rocky at that show, and later at my mom's place, my aunt finally convinced me it was a good idea—that I had something to offer.

"At the time, my parents had already divorced, and my dad was living in New Jersey. I called him up and said I was ready to go train. He said to quit my jobs and move up there. Within three weeks, I was training. When I got into the ring with my dad, it was just me and my dad. It wasn't me in the ring with a legend. A couple of things I noticed off the bat was he was a great teacher and very smooth. He took me through everything with baby steps. I've had many teachers I've been in the ring with at Ohio Valley Wrestling and WWE, but nobody went through it the way my dad did. And I'm not just saying that. He was very patient with me—more patient in the ring with me then he was at home. I gained so much respect for the business and all that my dad has accomplished when I started training. Before that, I didn't really respect what it took for him and the boys to do what they had done. Wrestling brought us closer."

—*Jimmy Snuka Jr.*

I moved to Las Vegas in 2001 to train Jimmy for a year. I put my life on hold for those 12 months, and it was worth it. He had natural instincts in the ring, and he wanted to be great. You have to want to be the best in order to be the best in this business. So, I trained him in New Jersey and at a wrestling school in Las Vegas, where I used to be a partner. Jimmy was working hard, was very dedicated, and got himself in great shape. He also was a good listener. When I told him something, he listened to what his old man had to say. He wanted to become a wrestler, and that's why he became a success in the WWE. He paid his dues and worked very hard to make it to the company.

When he got into the WWE as Deuce, I really believe he and Cliff Compton (aka Domino) made up one of the best tag teams ever. They just worked so well together in the ring, and I was so proud of my boy. I still am. I didn't care that he wrestled under Deuce and not Snuka. He made his own name for himself—just like I had done once upon a time. I loved tagging with my old friend Sgt. Slaughter against them at the Vengeance pay-per-view in 2007.

"The first match I had been in was the main event at an indie show with my dad versus Greg 'The Hammer' Valentine and Brutus Beefcake. I mean, that was my first match ever, and I'm in the ring with these three. I didn't have a clue. I went out as Jimmy Snuka Jr. and I was totally lost. I'd only been training for three months, and I was just so uncomfortable. My second match I changed my name to Solo, because I kind of wanted to be my own person.

"It was intimidating to me because of the way I grew up, but there were a lot of things I didn't know about the wrestling business. It never dawned on me to ask. I grew up in the locker room—Dwayne and I were always around it. Some of the stuff I found out from him. He told me about it. I was uncomfortable using the Snuka name, and Dwayne introduced me one night to Vince, and he told me not to use my dad's name either. I always remembered that. It was good for me to build up my own name.

"It took me four years to get the OVW contract. When I got to OVW, I got frustrated—I wanted to go up on the road, and I was watching everybody else getting called up. My dad was telling me to be patient and that my time would come. But I heard that for a long time, and I wasn't a very patient person. I got a lot of advice from Dwayne, my aunt Ata, and my dad, and they said to come up with something on my own. Domino was not under development yet, but he did this Andrew 'Dice' Clay thing. I saw him do that, and knew his whole schtick was a greaser, much like *The Outsiders* and the movie *Grease*, and I said, 'Wait a second, that's perfect!' My dad loved it."
—*Jimmy Snuka Jr.*

That Vengeance pay-per-view was one of the highlights of my career. It took place in Houston, Texas. I dove off the top rope for my son, which was hard for me to do because of my ankle

Me, Rocky, and Jimmy Jr.

and all, and I let him get out of it. I pulled him on top of me so he could get the pin. I loved it, brudda. The two of us were so pumped up for it. The plan was to start a feud on TV. We were supposed to have a few more matches, but as you may remember, that was the night Chris Benoit no-showed the event. We would all find out later that he killed his wife and young son and then himself. The WWE didn't know what to do next. Everyone was just in shock. The storyline with my son was never mentioned again. That Benoit situation was so terrible. I had been in the ring with him before, and he was such a great talent. He was one of the best wrestlers ever, but his legacy is tarnished forever.

It was just a tragic, tragic story. It makes me so sad to hear of wrestlers who die young. It happens way too much. It could have been me, brah. Had I not stopped using drugs, and had Carole not

Me and my daughter, Sarona

straightened me out, I could have been the one you read about in the newspapers. I was running so hard back in the 1980s—who knows where I would have ended up had I just kept going? Again, I am so thankful Carole came into my life, and I am so happy I was smart enough to stop using cocaine and steroids.

I am so proud of Jimmy Jr.'s wrestling career, and the same goes for my daughter Sarona and her career. She trained at Rocky Johnson's wrestling school, and I knew she had wanted to wrestle for a long time. She put it off for a while to start a family, but I knew she'd be back. I remember getting called into her school once when she was a teenager. The principal called to say Sarona was jumped by three other girls. They had picked a fight with her in the locker room. When I went to the principal's office, I thought he'd tell me some bad news—that Sarona was hurt. Instead, I found out she bloodied the girls and knocked them out. Once she started wrestling in the WWE as Tamina Snuka, I was able to watch her all the time, just like I watched Jimmy Jr. I would love to have a mixed-tag match with her one day.

> "I have got to be honest—at first, I loved working out with my dad and lifting weights and loved watching wrestling. But the older I got, I started to rebel against it, and I wanted to be the opposite of him. Even though the passion for wrestling and entertaining was still there! But after I did my path, it was time to fulfill what was always there. I remember when I first told Pops I was going to wrestle, he popped up and was so excited! He said, 'Let's do it, sista!' He never put it down. He stayed positive through the whole process."
> —Sarona Snuka-Polamalu

> "In a salute to her father, she wrestles as Tamina Snuka, but is often referred to as 'warrior goddess.' There is only one Superfly, but in her own right, Tamina has perfected the splash, Tamina-style! When she flies off of that top rope, one can only think... shades of the Superfly! Indeed, she is doing his legacy proud."
> —Ata Maivia Johnson

Both of my kids are good performers in the ring. They have natural instincts…as they should! I gave it all to them, brudda. They respect the business and respect what I have done, and they have made me so very proud by following in my footsteps.

Me and Dawn Marie

Wrestling is not an easy career to choose. It can be very hard to break in and to get it right. It's probably even harder to *stay* in the business. It's brutal, brah. I knew one young woman who was trying so hard to break into the business, I decided to take her under my wing. That's what the Superfly does sometimes—he sees something wrong and he makes it right. Dawn Marie is not a daughter of mine, but I helped her break into this business as much as I could. When the Superfly sees something in you, he backs you 100 percent. There was no question after I saw Dawn Marie at a show in New Jersey—I knew she belonged in this business.

"My first match ever was with Tony Atlas against Jimmy Snuka at an indie show in New Jersey in 1995 or 1996. Jimmy was watching me, and one day he just came up to me at an indie show, and he was like, 'I want you to manage me tonight, sista.' I was like, 'Wow...absolutely.' And he told me, 'No, you don't understand. You are the first woman I have ever let valet for me.' I couldn't believe it. It was a one-time deal, but it was such a gift. Later that night, he introduced me to [photographer] George Napolitano and Bill Apter, and he told them, 'Do me a personal favor, and make sure she's in every magazine.' He just helped me so much. I was in magazines constantly—it exposed me to the entire industry. He'd help me get bookings, and I'd do shows along New Jersey and up and down the East Coast.

"Ever since, he's been like a dad to me in this business. If I have a problem—professional or personal—he's someone I can always count on, and I know it's coming from a loving place. I was at a diner one time with him, we were sitting across from each other, and I just asked him, 'Why do you help me? You don't hit on me, you're never disrespectful to me...why do you do it?' And he said, 'Sista, because I see something special in you, and if I don't teach you my business, it ends with me, and it all means nothing.' At that time, I knew what he said was something great, but I didn't realize what he meant until later on. He gave me his business. This is a business that is given to you. You don't just go for lessons at a school and pay a couple thousand dollars and get in the business. You can do that and call yourself a wrestler, but the business is something that gets given to you.

"Jimmy is the most kind, gentle, understanding human being I've ever met in my life. He just has this amazing gift of making you feel you're whole."

—*Dawn Marie*

SAYING GOOD-BYE TO MOM AND A NEAR-DEATH EXPERIENCE

My mom's husband, Russell, eventually got sick, so my brother, Henry, put Mom in a nursing home in California, where he lived. She died on August 30, 1997. I got a call from my daughter, so I got a flight from Carole's house in New Jersey to California. Thankfully, I was able to see and talk to her in the hospital before she passed away. She was hooked up to all kinds of machines, but I think she knew it was me. She suffered from Alzheimer's disease and didn't understand much in the end. It was very hard to watch her become so forgetful. I know deep down that I made my mother proud. I still hold onto all of my memories of her. She was so important to me. As I have often said, she was my guardian angel, and I believe she is still looking after me from heaven.

Henry had her cremated and I have her ashes in my room. I guess you could say that she is still living with me.

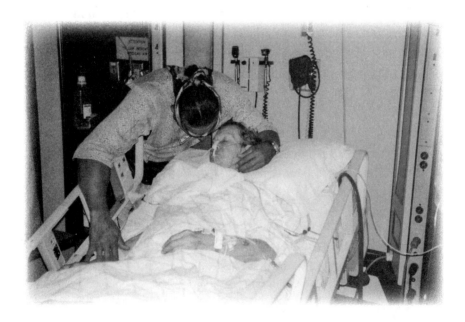

My life changed forever again in May of 2004. For the first time in my life, I was scared, brudda. One day, I just started feeling dizzy. I had eaten a tuna sandwich the day before, and I thought maybe I had food poisoning or something. I didn't want to scare Carole, so I didn't say anything to her. Later that night, though, I told her I was not feeling right.

The next day I still didn't feel well, but I played bocce ball with Carole's son Dennis anyway. I was not feeling myself at all—I felt a little light-headed and very out of sorts. Dennis got me some water, but I could barely stand.

> **"He started vomiting massive amounts of blood, and he passed out. I called the ambulance. When the ambulance came, there was blood everywhere. They took him to the ICU, and the first thing the nurse waiting on him said was, 'Jimmy, can I get your autograph before you get your tests?' That really scared us."**
> —*Carole Snuka*

The doctors said I had an ulcer. They said they fixed the problem by stopping the bleeding and cauterizing the damage over two days. They put me in a room, but I kept throwing up blood anyway. On the third day, they released me from the hospital.

> **"I called but they wouldn't give me any information because I wasn't married to him. They told me he was fine—that in 95 percent of the cases, patients were cured after that."**
> —*Carole Snuka*

They sent me home in my pajamas because I was too weak to dress myself. I remember going outside on the back porch and resting on a hammock. I had been home for three hours at that point, and I was talking to Liana, who was in Hawaii. The next thing I knew, I had dropped the phone and passed out again, brudda.

> **"Luckily I left work early, because he passed out again— blood was all over the place, and he lost control of his bowels. It looked like a crime scene. So, my daughter called the ambulance again."**
> —Carole Snuka

Carole says I was in another world while waiting for the ambulance. She said I thought I was at an autograph session or something, and that I had a strange look on my face. As soon as I stood up to meet the paramedics, I hit the ground again.

People say that you see a light when you are near death. Well, the Superfly saw it, brudda. When I was in the ambulance, I remember feeling totally relaxed. I closed my eyes, and I saw a bright light moving farther and farther away from me—it was like I was in a tunnel. I remember hearing the paramedic yell at the driver to go faster because "we're losing him." Carole was yelling, "Don't you dare leave me, bub!" I just said to her "Shhh, I'm okay." I think her yelling woke me up—it was louder than any siren, brudda!

I kept vomiting when we got to the hospital. Carole said I was throwing up huge clots of blood—enough to fill bedpans, brah! She said they pumped my stomach with syringes of water, and the more they pumped, the more blood I threw up.

> "They got to the point where they had to intubate him. He was going. They made me leave the room, and the nurses were running up and down the hallway with bags of blood. They were transfusing him as fast as they could, and he kept vomiting it out. It was hours before they had stabilized him enough to do more surgery. They had never cauterized his stomach as they said. They removed a chunk of his stomach. The problem was the ulcer in his stomach had eaten through the lining and hit an artery. Later that night, they put him in intensive care. His body swelled all over, and he was hallucinating."
> —Carole Snuka

I was totally out of my mind. Carole told me I pulled out all the tubes connected to me, including the catheter, and tried to go home. The doctors came and stopped me. I was lucky I didn't damage myself even more. I was told I could've really screwed things up.

It took me almost a year to get right, brah. There were times I didn't think I was going to make it. I remember after leaving the hospital that second time, it still felt like I had to expend a ton of energy just to open up my eyes. God bless Carole, brudda. She took care of me. After I came home, she had to change the dressings and wipe away the area around my stomach. I couldn't eat. I got down under 100 pounds. I was just skin and bones, brah.

> "It was two months after his surgery and he still was not walking or eating. I saw white strings [of gauze] coming out of his stomach, and the doctors told me it was nothing. We changed to my family doctor. They treated him differently—they gave him

testosterone and opened him up and started fishing around in there. They checked his stomach and found a ruler-sized piece of gauze in his stomach. The doctor said, 'I don't think he'll have any problems anymore.' The bad smell that was coming from his stomach went away, and he started to eat again."
—*Carole Snuka*

But I still was not out of the woods, brudda. I had aspirated into a lung and couldn't breathe, so that was another week in the hospital. After four months, I finally felt I was ready to wrestle again. I had missed it so much, and I was so happy to be alive. After going through all that, Carole and I decided to get married. We shared everything together, and she had saved my life. It seemed right to take the next step.

"We had no intention of getting married. Jimmy even promised his kids he wasn't going to get married. Then he got really sick, and I asked him, 'What are we afraid of?'"
—*Carole Snuka*

But before the year was out, I was back in the hospital. I had been wrestling but noticed that my stomach looked like it was growing. I ignored it at first, but eventually it got to be the size of a basketball. I looked pregnant! It turned out I had a hernia and an infection from the surgery. I was getting very, very sick again. I remember having to wear long shirts to cover up my stomach, which I learned had swelled because my intestines were pressing against my skin. But I told Carole to keep booking me anyway.

Wrestling is my life—I was not going to spend more time away from the ring than I already had. Eventually, I had surgery.

After the hernia operation, the doctor asked me to stop jumping off the ropes. I said, "Brudda, that's what people come to see." Carole suggested I jump from the second rope, but I resisted. It was not until my ankle really started giving out that I finally went down a step when I did the Superfly splash. I've been pretty healthy since.

Nearly dying made me realize how important life is, brudda. So, I try to take good care of myself now. I still like to have my medicine—I'll still smoke some pot but I've cut down on cigarettes. Anyone who knows me in this business knows how much I used to smoke!

GETTING MARRIED AGAIN AND LOVING MY FAMILY

Carole and I have a great time together, brudda. She takes care of me, and I do my best to take care of her. At first, we weren't interested in getting married again. We just had fun dating each other and getting to know one another. We both had been in difficult marriages, so we weren't in any hurry to put a label on what we were. We just enjoyed each other's company. But things changed when I got sick. I realized that life is short and that we were ready to trust again. There used to be a time when women would follow the Superfly around. Now, my wife goes everywhere with me. There is no hanky panky going on, and I'm fine with that.

> "The best thing that happened to him is Carole.
> I hate to think what would've happened to Jimmy
> had someone not taken over. She saved him."
> —Tito Santana

We were married September 4, 2004, which is Carole's birthday. Like I've said, my memory is not what it once was, so it's nice to have one date to remember for both our anniversary and her birthday, brudda! It was a second chance for the Superfly, even though it was my third marriage.

We had an outdoor, Hawaiian-style wedding. Everyone was encouraged to dress in Hawaiian clothes, and Carole and I made the leis for all the women in the wedding party. The flowers came from Hawaii. We painted shells with glitter and hung white lights all around the yard of Carole's daughter, Bridget. Her husband made a gazebo for the ceremony.

I know it took Carole some time to track down Sharon and my divorce papers for the license, but she did. Carole's daughter was the matron of honor, and Carole's granddaughters were flower girls. My brother was supposed to be the best man, but he was late to the wedding, so it wound up being Carole's son.

"When Henry arrived, I said hello and gave him some food.
The first thing he said to me was, 'Now Jimmy has been
married as many times as me.' I said, 'Oh yeah, how many
times have you been married?' And he said, 'Three.' I walked
out to Jimmy and gave him the 'come here' sign. He came in
and I asked him how many times he had been married, and he
said, 'Two. You are the third.' I said, 'Didn't you think that was
an important thing to tell me?' He said, 'No, it didn't work out.'
Needless to say, I didn't talk to him for a while."
—Carole Snuka

I invited my family but they didn't come. It's taken a while for
my children to warm up to Carole. She never wanted to replace
their mother, but I understand if they felt that way or feel that
way today. I always said I would never get married again because the last marriage was so hard. But I loved Carole so much
and it felt like the right thing to do. We had been through so
much together, and she saved me. She is a kind and caring person. I am a better man today because of my "bub."

"I recently bonded with Carole and got to know her.
I really do respect her."
—Ata Snuka Campbell

It upset me that my family didn't come to the wedding, but
I understood where they were coming from. I just felt I should
be happy, too. Carole made me very happy. She treats me and
everyone else with so much kindness. She let her ex-husband's
mother live with us. She was a good person. I didn't mind going

to the store for her or talking to her. After she passed away, Carole's mother moved in, and then Henry moved in after that. We were never alone, which was a little crazy, but opening up our home was the right thing to do.

We went to Hawaii after our wedding and visited Liana and Sarona. We had a lovely time at the beach and playing in the pool with my grandkids. It doesn't get better than that, brah.

> "My dad is a great father. It was all about the kids as soon as he came home. We loved when he came home—anything he could think of he would do for fun to make up for the days he wasn't there. I remember we could never eat when he took us anywhere. We'd go to restaurants, and people would be around him all the time. My dad would sometimes wait to take us late so there wouldn't be as many people there or he'd buy a restaurant out for the night so we could eat in peace and just be by ourselves."
> —Liana Snuka

PROBLEMS WITH DRINKING

> "Jimmy is like a brother to me and always will be, but when he's drinking he is a pain in the butt."
> —Rocky Johnson

I was told that when I drank, I could be mean, arrogant, and stubborn. I was not violent, but I was not nice to be around. I didn't know I was rude back then, so I apologize to anyone I ever treated badly. The Superfly doesn't like to be disrespectful to anybody. I can admit now that I had a problem with drinking, but I couldn't for many, many years. I am an alcoholic. Every wrestler back in the day would drink, and I don't mean just a little. The boys would drink tons of alcohol. I've been told I was a real bastard whenever I drank a lot. It was not until about five years ago, though, that I had to quit. I had always thought of drinking as a habit—not an addiction. But that was not true.

> **"He's one of the all-time greats and a great human being...**
> **He's the most peaceful, calmest guy—until he drinks."**
> —Ric Flair

> **"I always knew to stay away from Jimmy when he was drinking.**
> **He was a happy, fall-on-your-face drunk, but he needed someone**
> **to put him to bed. He just partied too much."**
> —Bill Apter

The WWE has a great wellness policy, and I went for a four-day evaluation in Atlanta five years ago. But I really didn't want to stop drinking, so I left. That's when I realized for sure that I had a problem. Plus, I wrestled two shows drunk around that time, something I had never done before. I was really bad in the ring and ended up apologizing to the promoter later.

It was my health that got me to stop cold turkey. See, it's always difficult to stop drinking when you're in this business. Booze is all around you. Everyone wants to party with the Superfly—it doesn't matter if I'm 70 years old or 20. It's always been the same. The drinks just come. I say no, but they end up sitting in front of me anyway. But one night in Las Vegas, I was doing a show and I passed out, brudda. I felt sick to my stomach, and everything went black.

I felt a similar sickness the next few times I went drinking. I also started bruising more easily. I really knew something was wrong after I felt light-headed following a match I had against Chris Jericho leading up to WrestleMania 25. When I went to the doctor the next day, they ran some tests and I found out I had diabetes. My blood sugar was 580, brudda. Dr. Costa knew me well and said I should be in the hospital, but he also knew I wouldn't do well in there. So, he worked very closely with me and we got it under control, though I did lose a lot of weight. I also had to stop drinking, and that was very hard for me.

Now when I drink, my blood sugar drops and sometimes I can get dizzy and fall down. So, I try not to drink much anymore. My doctor still tells me to be careful, but I tell him, "Brudda, I know what I'm doing. I'll be okay." I'll still have a drink on occasion, but it makes me feel sick, so most times I don't bother. I'm still always around alcohol, and it's so hard to stay away from it. People never take no for answer. They still want to buy me drinks even when I don't want them. Back in the day, I'd always go out drinking with the boys after the show at a party or a bar. Now, I can't drink when I want to drink.

> "He's become very humble and soft-spoken. It comes with age. He's learned so much."
> —Matt Borne

A NEW BEGINNING WITH A BLESSED FAMILY

I love my wife, Carole, my children, and all of my grandchildren. Carole's children feel just like my own. I love them and my whole family from all over. I love you all for reading this book. I'm so very proud of my children in particular. I keep in touch with them and am proud of the beautiful homes they have. I'm so grateful for the grandkids they gave to me—they are a true blessing. My job is to make sure they all continue to do the right thing, and I'll make sure of it. I'm not gone yet, brudda!

If I ever do retire, I just want to go to Hawaii or the Fiji Islands and sit on a beach. Maybe I'll climb up a coconut tree and throw down some coconuts. Maybe I'll have a drink and just talk to the heavenly father. I don't know.

I live my life in the present, and a word like *retirement* doesn't fit in my vocabulary. The love I have for wrestling is still there. If you asked me what I'd be doing before my last match, I'd say I'd be preparing myself for the next match. There is no end in sight. As long as the Superfly can fly, that's exactly what I'm going to do, no matter what. I'm going to fly again, brudda.

When this brudda isn't around anymore, they will say he was the one and only Superfly, and there can never be another one. He tried to live a good life and enjoy what God gave him. He had his demons and tried to overcome them in order to teach others how to love the way God loves us. He never met a person he didn't like or love. He tried to find the good in everyone.

I think I was put on this earth to be a missionary, to spread the word, and to teach people how to love one another. Rich or poor, we are all God's children. I don't judge people for their weaknesses and hope they will not judge me for mine. Like I always say, treat all bruddas and sistas the way you want them to treat you. I hope I have made my people proud of me. *Vinaka vaka levu!* (That means "thank you very much" in Fijian!)

"When I was a child growing up, my mom talked about how one day she wanted to go to Hawaii. It was a dream of hers that she talked about all the time, and I used to tell her that when I was older, I would take her. I can't help but think now that this longing she had for Hawaii was actually the universe wanting to bring together two people who are truly soul mates. I've never seen a couple have so much fun together, from the cute jokes they play on one another to the funny nicknames they call each other. They really just enjoy each other's company, and are always laughing and having a good time. Their love runs as deep as the ocean.

"Jimmy is the most patient, understanding, and forgiving person I know. Nothing seems to make him mad or stressed out—it's almost like he lives by the motto in *The Lion King*, 'hakuna matata.' Even though I was an adult when I met Jimmy, he still had that fatherly instinct toward me. He enjoyed trying to scare my dates, which he now continues to do with any boy my daughter brings around.

"My daughter and Jimmy have a special bond. He does not call her by her first name—he calls her Star. He's been a part of her life since the day she was born, and we lived with my mom and Jimmy for the first five years of her life. In actuality, he's helped raise her. He used to jokingly tell me, 'Sister, have another, because this one's ours.' My husband and Jimmy have become close friends. There's something about Jimmy when he's trying to give you advice: he tends to start off strong, and halfway through he'll have you confused. But by the end, he leaves you thinking, *Wow, that was deep, I totally get his message.* Jimmy was also one of the first people to get my youngest daughter, who suffers from autism, to engage and interact with someone. This was due to the patience he had with her. I could go on forever saying wonderful things about Jimmy. We feel truly blessed to have him in our lives."

—Bridget Martinovitch, Carole's daughter

EPILOGUE

"I just recently wrestled at an indie show and there he was—nearly 70 years old, and he still looks good. He still works really hard."
—*Tommy Dreamer*

Hello again, all you people in TV wonderland! It is March of 2012, and I have just had my cast removed. I am walking around with a boot on my foot and am able to get around on my own. My ankle is not quite healed yet, brudda, but it's getting there. I can put pressure on it, and I am getting closer to seeing you all in that ring again. The doctor said I am going to need to keep the boot on until I start training to get back in the ring. I can see the finish line, brudda. As soon as this heals up and the doctors give me the go-ahead, the Superfly will be ready to enter the ring and see all you lovely people again. My ankle is doing better than even I thought it would be. There is no pain.

Brudda, I was in such pain before I had my ankle done. I was grumpy, because I could not even work in my yard. Remember, I like to be outside in the beautiful nature! I put the surgery off for so long, but the body tells you when it's ready, and my ankle quit on me. My brudda Dr. Raikin from the Rothman Institute is the very best there is. I had my surgery at Jefferson Hospital in Philadelphia, and he worked his magic on my ankle. I go to therapy three times a week now and work with Dr. Charles Sacco. He is working me pretty hard, but it feels so good. I love that feeling, brudda. I told him that I plan on getting back into the ring, and he said, "I don't know, Jimmy." But I know what this body can do, and I feel better than ever. I quit smoking and drinking, and thank the good Lord for helping me quit. I pray every day that He will help me stay this way. It's still hard to be around someone who smokes—when I smell that smell, I want to grab a smoke myself, but I have to fight it. But my whole life has been a fight, hasn't it?

I thank Carole, my guardian angel, my best friend, and my wife, for her support. I should be out of this boot in a few weeks, and then down to an air cast and eventually back to my bare feet again. Like I said, I know I'm not done. I will probably die in that ring before calling it quits. I was put on this planet to wrestle.

Sure, I've looked back in this book, but I'm also looking forward. I enjoy what I do. I love it so much that I'm just going to keep going. When I think about everything that's happened in my life, how could I *not* keep going? I want to get back in the ring with the kids in WWE and show them how it's done. There's no psychology anymore. Everything goes too fast, and it's the same thing over and over. Why don't they change things around a little bit? You never see me come in and have the same match. Something is always going to be different.

Being in the ring still gives me goose bumps. I love my fans and I miss them. The Superfly is going to fly again sooner than you think, brudda. As a matter of fact, by the time this book comes out, I'll probably have splashed someone in a wrestling ring near you.

AFTERWORD

I ran across an article one day while doing some reading, and I liked it so much, I cut it out and tacked it on the wall of my cubicle at work. It was written by Maya Angelou, and she said, "You can tell a lot about a person by the way they handle three things: rainy days, lost luggage, and tangled Christmas lights." I really thought it over, and remembered how I threw out old Christmas lights because I would get so frustrated with them. How many people have the patience to sit and untangle Christmas lights? Well, I found one. And not only did I find a person who could be patient with Christmas lights, but I also found someone who loves the rain. Jimmy calls rain a blessing from God. He does not sit inside and pout because he can't work outside. He enjoys every day of his life. He showers himself in the rain and embraces it. It's almost like the rain rejuvenates him.

I often pick Jimmy up at the airport when he's coming home from a long trip, and he is usually tired and hungry. He just wants to get home and have a good meal. Well, one time Jimmy's luggage was lost when he changed flights. We waited at least an hour until they tracked it down. It was somewhere on the West Coast. He just said, "Okay, let me know when you get it."

He signed autographs for all the people working for the airline, gave them hugs, and said good night. I said, "Aren't you mad that they lost your luggage?" He said, "It's not their fault, they are just doing their jobs. And it's just luggage, no worries!" The luggage arrived the next night, and I learned something from Jimmy. Why worry and get upset over something I can't change?

Jimmy wanted to surprise me one Christmas, so he and my son went to a tree farm and cut down a tree for me. I usually pick the same kind of tree every year. I know just the kind I like, and I decorate it the same way every season. Well, this one year Jimmy picked a tree that I would have *never* picked! It was skinny, short, and not very full. I didn't know how to react. I thought it might be a joke, but I didn't want to take a chance and hurt his feelings. Either way, it was the thought that counted. I didn't know how we could make this tree look good. Jimmy started to untangle the Christmas tree lights and I thought, *Here we go, get ready to go buy more lights.* Well, he sat on the sofa for *hours* untangling those lights. He didn't complain at all. He just took his time, we talked like nothing was wrong, and eventually I forgot what he was even doing. I used my imagination and decorated the tree with ornaments, ribbon, and red and white poinsettias with gold trim. It was my best-looking tree ever. Who would have thought that skinny little tree would look so good? We had fun, felt no stress, and enjoyed the entire process—just the way it should be.

I glance at that clipping I tacked up in my cubicle so many years ago and realize that I have met a very unique person. This is someone I want in my life; this is someone I wish I could be more like. He calms me when I'm uptight, makes me laugh when I'm down, and slows me down when I'm running around like a nut. He loves me unconditionally. He tells me how good I look just after I've scrubbed the bathroom. He has helped me

through double hip-replacement surgery, and even got a maintenance man at the hospital to go into storage and get me a better mattress.

We take care of each other, and I know that sometimes I go overboard, but it's out of love. I don't know what I would ever do without him. He always tells me, "We are a team, and a team sticks together and looks out for one another."

Sometimes I wonder if Maya Angelou was thinking about Jimmy Snuka when she wrote those words. I know she wasn't, but she did describe him to a T. He is a wonderful person trying his best to be a good man.

—Carole Snuka

APPENDIX

THE JIMMY SNUKA TIMELINE

1970—Jimmy begins wrestling in Hawaii

1971—Jimmy begins wrestling in Portland and makes his debut in Japan

1972—Jimmy joins AWA and teams with Don Muraco. He takes on everyone from Dusty Rhodes to Ivan Koloff

1973–77—Jimmy returns to Portland and competes in first NWA championship matches

February 19 and March 4, 1974—Jimmy wrestles two 60-minute matches with world champion Jack Brisco

1977—Jimmy wrestles for Fritz Von Erich in Texas

1978—Jimmy returns to Portland and then leaves for Mid-Atlantic Wrestling aka Jim Crockett Promotions

November 1978—Jimmy debuts with Paul Orndorff, and the tag team defeats Baron Von Raschke and Greg "The Hammer" Valentine in a non-title match. They would later win the tag team titles

1978–81—Jimmy wrestles for Mid-Atlantic Wrestling

June–September 1981—Jimmy wrestles in Georgia Championship Wrestling and later holds tag team titles with Terry Gordy

Winter 1981—Jimmy tags with Bruiser Brody for All Japan
Wrestling

December 1981—Jimmy and Brody win the "Real World Tag
Team Championship" tournament

January–March 1982—Jimmy wrestles in Oklahoma before
leaving for the WWF

1982–85—Jimmy wrestles in WWF; highlights include feuds
with Don Muraco, Bob Backlund, and Rowdy Roddy Piper

June 28, 1982—Jimmy Snuka climbs to the top of a 15-foot-
high steel cage in front of a sold-out crowd at Madison

Square Garden. He misses WWF heavyweight champion Bob
Backlund…barely

May–December 1985—Jimmy works for New Japan Wrestling
and in Hawaii

1986–87—Jimmy returns to the AWA and wrestles in Memphis
while continuing to wrestle in Japan

1987–88—Jimmy wrestles for All Japan Wrestling

1989–92—Jimmy returns to WWF

1992–94—Jimmy wrestles for ECW and becomes its first
champion

September 27, 1993—Jimmy defeats Paul Van Dale on *Monday
Night RAW*

1994–Present—Jimmy continues to perform on the independent
wrestling circuit

November 16, 1996—Jimmy is inducted into the WWE Hall of
Fame

NOTABLE MATCHES
1971

July 23: Medford, OR—Jimmy and Cowboy Frankie Laine defeat Johnny Boyd and Norman F. Charles III (Won the Pacific
Northwest tag team titles)

September 1: Los Angeles, CA—Jimmy and Suni War Cloud
defeat El Solitario and El Gran Goliath

November 13: Honolulu, HI—Jimmy defeats Mr. Fuji

November 24: Honolulu, HI—Jimmy wrestles The Destroyer to
a draw

December 25: Honolulu, HI—Jimmy wrestles with Sam
Steamboat against Mighty Brutus and Dingo the Sundowner

1972

February 19: Honolulu, HI—Jimmy defeats Mad Dog Vachon

May 3: Honolulu, HI—Jimmy wrestles Curtis Iaukea to a draw

September 22: Denver, CO—Jimmy defeats Ivan Koloff

October 7: Minneapolis, MN—Jimmy and Don Muraco defeat Larry Hennig and Dusty Rhodes

November 11: Milwaukee, WI—Jimmy and Don Muraco defeat Rene Goulet and Bobby Heenan

December 26: Moline, IL—Jimmy loses to Larry Hennig

1973

April 17: Honolulu, HI—Jimmy loses to Tony Borne by disqualification

May 16: Honolulu, HI—Jimmy and Sam Steamboat defeat Lars Anderson and Mad Dog Vachon

October 27: Portland, OR—Jimmy and Dutch Savage defeat Bull Ramos and Ripper Collins (Won the Pacific Northwest tag team title (2))

November 16: Eugene, OR—Jimmy defeats Bull Ramos (Won the Pacific Northwest heavyweight title)

December 26: Portland, OR—Jimmy defeats Greg Valentine

1974

January 12: Portland, OR—Jimmy loses to Ripper Collins (Lost the Pacific Northwest title)

February 2: Portland, OR—Jimmy teams with Andre the Giant, co-won a battle royal

February 19: Portland, OR—Jimmy wrestles NWA world champion Jack Brisco to a draw

November 9: Portland, OR—Jimmy defeats Bob Remus, aka
  Sgt. Slaughter
December 2: Kagoshima, Japan—Jimmy loses to The Destroyer

1975

February 15: Portland, OR—Jimmy defeats Tor Kamata
July 16: Seattle, WA—Jimmy loses to NWA world champion
  Jack Brisco
October 6: Vancouver, BC—Jimmy and Dennis Stamp defeat
  Gene Kiniski and Dale Lewis

October 7: Portland, OR—Jimmy wrestles Jesse Ventura to a draw

December 22: Vancouver, BC—Jimmy loses to Gene Kiniski

1976

January 17: Portland, OR—Jimmy loses to Jesse Ventura (Lost the Pacific Northwest title)

April 12: Vancouver, BC—Jimmy and Don Leo Jonathan defeat Gene Kiniski and Seigfried Steinke (Won the Canadian tag team titles)

September 11: Portland, OR—Jimmy defeats Jesse Ventura in a Fijian death match

October 15: Portland, OR—Jimmy wrestles NWA world champion Terry Funk to a draw

December 7: Portland, OR—Jimmy, Afa, and Sika defeat Kurt Von Hess, Pat O'Brien, and Randy Morse

1977

February 26: Portland, OR—Jimmy defeats Buddy Rose

March 19 Portland, OR—Jimmy and Jay Youngblood wrestle Jesse Ventura and Buddy Rose to a draw

May 20: Houston, TX—Jimmy defeats El Gran Goliath (Won the Texas heavyweight title)

September 13: Portland, OR—Jimmy wrestles NWA world champion Harley Race to a draw

November 7: Fort Worth, TX—Jimmy and David Von Erich defeat Bull Ramos and John Studd

1978

January 25: Seattle, WA—Jimmy defeats Gino Hernandez

February 11: Portland, OR—Jimmy loses to The Iron Sheik

February 15: Seattle, WA—Jimmy and Jesse Ventura lose to Buddy Rose and Ed Wiskowski

August 19: San Francisco, CA—Jimmy defeats Roddy Piper

December 26: Richmond, VA—Jimmy and Paul Orndorff defeat Greg Valentine and Baron Von Raschke (Won the NWA World tag team titles)

1979

January 8: Greenville, SC—Jimmy and Paul Orndorff defeat Ric Flair and Greg Valentine

February 11: Greensboro, NC—Jimmy defeats Ric Flair

April 1: Greensboro, NC—Jimmy won a two-ring battle royal

September 1: Charlotte, NC—Jimmy defeats Ricky Steamboat (Won the vacant NWA United States title)

December 30: Toronto, ON—Jimmy and Ray Stevens defeat Ric Flair and Dewey Robertson

1980

April 20: Greensboro, NC—Jimmy loses to Ric Flair (Lost the NWA United States title)

June 2: Greenville, SC—Jimmy and The Iron Sheik lose to Matt Borne and Buzz Sawyer

June 8: Greensboro, NC—Jimmy and The Iron Sheik defeat Ric Flair and Greg Valentine in a cage match

June 22: Greensboro, NC—Jimmy and Ray Stevens defeat Ricky Steamboat and Jay Youngblood (Won the NWA World tag team titles (2))

November 27: Greensboro, NC—Jimmy and Ray Stevens lose to Masked Superstar and Paul Jones in a cage match (Lost the NWA World tag team titles)

1981

February 22: Toronto, ON—Jimmy defeats Mad Dog Vachon

April 13 Brantford, ON—Jimmy and Roddy Piper defeat Ric Flair and Angelo Mosca by disqualification

May 23: Tokyo, Japan—Jimmy and The Sheik lose to Ricky Steamboat and Jumbo Tsuruta

July 6: Augusta, GA—Jimmy and Terry Gordy defeat Ted DiBiase and Steve O (Won the National tag team titles)

December 13: Tokyo, Japan—Jimmy and Bruiser Brody defeat Terry and Dory Funk Jr. (Won AJPW Real World tag league tournament)

1982

April 26: New York, NY—Jimmy defeats WWF world champion Bob Backlund by disqualification

June 28: New York, NY—Jimmy loses to WWF world champion Bob Backlund in a steel cage match

October 8: Pittsburgh, PA—Jimmy defeats Curt Hennig

November 22: New York, NY—Jimmy defeats Lou Albano

December 26: Worcester, MA—Jimmy and Rocky Johnson defeat Ray Stevens and Lou Albano

1983

February 10: Altoona, PA—Jimmy defeats Superstar Billy Graham

March 19: Philadelphia, PA—Jimmy, Andre the Giant, and Bob Backlund defeat John Studd, Lou Albano, and Afa

September 17: Los Angeles, CA—Jimmy defeats Don Muraco by disqualification (guest referee: Tito Santana)

October 17: New York, NY—Jimmy loses to Don Muraco in a steel cage match

December 26: New York, NY—Jimmy and Arnold Skaaland defeat Don Muraco and Lou Albano

1984

January 16: St. Louis, MO—Jimmy is presented with the 1983 Wrestler of the Year Award during match with Israel Matia

February 3: White Plains, NY—Jimmy and Bob Backlund defeat Afa and Sika

June 23: Baltimore, MD—Jimmy and Andre the Giant defeat Dick Murdoch and Adrian Adonis by disqualification

July 20: St. Louis, MO—Jimmy defeats Roddy Piper in a Fijian strap match

December 28: New York, NY—Jimmy and Tonga Kid wrestle
Roddy Piper and Bob Orton Jr. to a double-disqualification

1985

January 21: New York, NY—Jimmy and Junkyard Dog lose to
Roddy Piper and Bob Orton Jr. in a tornado match

February 9: Landover, MD—Jimmy and Blackjack Mulligan defeat Brutus Beefcake and Johnny Valiant

March 31: New York, NY—Jimmy appears at WrestleMania I in
Hulk Hogan and Mr. T's corner for their match against Roddy
Piper and Paul Orndorff (with Bob Orton Jr. at ringside)

August 3: Honolulu, HI—Jimmy defeats Larry Sharpe

December 6: Tokyo, Japan—Jimmy and Bruiser Brody defeat
Dick Murdoch and Masked Superstar by count-out

1986

April 20: Minneapolis, MN—Jimmy and Greg Gagne defeat
  Nord the Barbarian and Bruiser Brody in a steel cage match

June 29: Denver, CO—Jimmy, Verne Gagne, and Greg Gagne
  defeat Boris Zhukov, Nord the Barbarian, and Adnan
  Al-Kaissie

July 19: Honolulu, HI—Jimmy and Rocky Johnson lose to The
  Blonds

August 16: Pittsburgh, PA—Jimmy defeats Larry Zbyzsko

October 19: St. Paul, MN—Jimmy defeats Boris Zhukov

1987

March 2: Memphis, TN—Jimmy and J.T. Southern defeat
  Tarzan Goto and Mr. Rising Sun (Won the CWA International
  tag team titles)

March 28: Wausau, WI—Jimmy defeats Col. DeBeers in a steel
    cage match

April 3: Waukesha, WI—Jimmy, Shawn Michaels, and Marty
    Jannetty defeat Doug Somers, Boris Zhukov, and Kevin Kelly

November 22: Tokyo, Japan—Jimmy and Bruiser Brody lose to
    Stan Hansen and Terry Gordy

December 11: Tokyo, Japan—Jimmy and Bruiser Brody lose to
    Jumbo Tsuruta and Yoshiaki Yatsu

1988

April 21: Tokyo, Japan—Jimmy and Bruiser Brody defeat John
    Tenta and Yoshiaki Yatsu

August 29: Tokyo, Japan—Jimmy and Johnny Ace defeat Tiger
    Mask and Shinichi Nakano

August 30: Osaka, Japan—Jimmy and Abdullah the Butcher
    wrestle Stan Hansen and Tom Zenk to a draw

September 9: Chiba, Japan—Jimmy and Tom Zenk defeat Isao
    Takagi and Akira Taue

September 15: Tokyo, Japan—Jimmy and Tiger Mask defeat
    Great Kabuki and Akio Sato

1989

March 8: Odessa, TX—Jimmy defeats Brooklyn Brawler

April 2: Atlantic City—Jimmy appears but does not wrestle at
    WrestleMania V

June 16: Los Angeles, CA—Jimmy defeats The Honky Tonk Man

August 28: East Rutherford, NJ—Jimmy loses to Ted DiBiase by
    count-out

September 21: Cincinnati, OH—Jimmy loses to Randy Savage

October 28: New York, NY—Jimmy loses to Mr. Perfect

1990

April 1: Toronto, ON—Jimmy loses to Rick Rude at
    WrestleMania VI

April 13: Tokyo, Japan—Jimmy and Tito Santana defeat Kenta
    Kobashi and Masa Fuchi

June 8: East Rutherford, NJ—Jimmy defeats Akeem

October 13: San Francisco, CA—Jimmy defeats The Genius

December 29: Cincinnati, OH—Jimmy defeats Haku

1991

March 16: Pittsburgh, PA—Jimmy loses to The Mountie

March 24: Los Angeles, CA—Jimmy loses to The Undertaker at
    WrestleMania VII

April 22: New York, NY—Jimmy loses to Irwin R. Shyster

September 30: Wheeling, WV—Jimmy, Kerry Von Erich, and
    Greg Valentine defeat Pat Tanaka and Beau and Blake Beverly

December 14: Honolulu, HI—Jimmy defeats Rick Martel

1992

January 31: New York, NY—Jimmy loses to Shawn Michaels

April 25: Tabor, PA—Jimmy defeats Salvatore Bellomo (Won
    the first ECW heavyweight title)

April 26: Philadelphia, PA—Jimmy loses to Johnny Hotbody
    (Loses the ECW heavyweight title)

July 14: Philadelphia, PA—Jimmy defeats Johnny Hotbody
    (Won the ECW heavyweight title (2))

September 30: Philadelphia, PA—Jimmy loses to Don Muraco
    (Loses the ECW heavyweight title)

1993

March 12: Radnor, PA—Jimmy defeats Glenn Osborne (Won the
ECW Television title)

May 23: Jimmy, Don Muraco, and Dick Murdoch wrestle
Wahoo McDaniel, Blackjack Mulligan, and Jim Brunzell to a
no-contest in World Championship Wrestling (WCW)

September 25: New York, NY—Jimmy defeats Brian
Christopher (WWF)

October 1: Philadelphia, PA—Jimmy, Don Muraco, and Kevin
Sullivan lose to Abdullah the Butcher, Terry Funk, and J.T. Smith

October 1: Philadelphia, PA—Jimmy loses to Terry Funk (Loses
the ECW Television title)

1994

February 5: Philadelphia, PA—Jimmy defeats Tommy Dreamer

March 26: Valley Forge, PA—Jimmy defeats Tommy Dreamer in a steel cage match

July 15: Philadelphia, PA—Jimmy and The Pitbulls lose to Tommy Dreamer, Terry Funk, and Dory Funk Jr.

July 17: Wildwood, NJ—Jimmy loses to Shane Douglas

August 13: Philadelphia, PA—Jimmy and The Tazmaniac defeat The Pitbulls

1996

November 17: New York, NY—Jimmy, Savio Vega, Yokozuna, and Flash Funk wrestle Ron Simmons, Vader, Diesel II (Glen Jacobs), and Razor Ramon II (Rick Bogner) to a draw

2000

January 10: Buffalo, NY—Jimmy defeats Jeff Jarrett in a cage match on WCW *Monday Night Nitro*. Chris Benoit serves as guest referee and hits Jarrett with a head butt from the top of cage

2001

November 2001: Orlando, FL—Jimmy manages his son, Jimmy Snuka Jr., at the first and only set of XWF shows at Universal Studios

November 7, 2004: Orlando, FL—Jimmy appears on the first TNA PPV, Victory Road, and is a guest on Piper's Pit. Piper apologizes for hitting him with a coconut and asks him to get revenge by hitting him with one. Jimmy doesn't. Kid Kash, Frankie Zazarian, and Michael Shane attack Snuka. Sonjay Dutt comes to Jimmy's aid, but he is hit with a coconut.

2005

November 1: San Diego, CA—Back with WWE, Jimmy and Eugene defeat Rob Conway and Tyson Tomko

2007

June 24: Houston, TX—Jimmy and Sgt. Slaughter loses to Deuce, aka Jimmy's son, and Domino

2009

April 5, 2009: Houston, TX—Jimmy taps out to Chris Jericho at WrestleMania XXV during a handicap match. Jericho also defeats Roddy Piper and Ricky Steamboat

APPENDIX

THE SNUKA FAMILY TREE

CHILDREN/GRANDCHILDREN

Jimmy Snuka Jr. (Arizona)
    Panina
    Jamesa
    Onis
    Sarona
Liana Snuka Laulu (Hawaii)
    Lia
    Fili
    Snuka
Sarona Snuka (Florida)
    Milinetta
    Maleata
Ata Snuka Campbell (Arizona)
    Siane

STEPCHILDREN

Bridget Maston Martinovitch
    Carlye
    Cammye
Richard Maston (Florida)
    Richie
    Kaitlyn
    Gabriela
Dennis Maston (Florida)
    Hunter
    Tucker

FAMILY NICKNAMES

Carole: Bubby
Penina: Tiger Penian
Jamesa: Tiger Jamesa
Onis: Tiger O
Sarona: Losana
Fili: Lion King
Milaneta: Salt
Maleata: Pepper
Carlye: My Star
Hunter: Tiger
Cammye: Curly
(Siane, Tucker, and Gabriela were born in 2011 and do not have their nicknames yet)

APPENDIX
THE SNUK-TIONARY

Many times, I take words and make them my own, no matter what the real meanings or pronunciations of the words are. Some are Fijian and Hawaiian words, others are just words and phrases I've made up. Feel free to use them yourself, brudda!

Broke da mouth: Hawaiian pidgin way of saying something tastes so good that my mouth is broken

Gimmick: When I can't remember the name of something, I call it a gimmick. For example, Pat Patterson was a gimmick.

Tooths: teeth

Ponths: pants

Feets: feet

Truts: truth

Lolo: Fijian for crazy

Pakalolo: Marijuana

Cockroach: To take or steal from somebody

You're ringin' my ear bells: That's what I say if someone's talking too loud

On the Kinny Popo: You hit the nail right on the head

Wiki-Wiki: What I say when I get up in the morning or do something that hurts

Grind: Eat

Kanaka: Island brother

ACKNOWLEDGMENTS

We would like to thank Triumph Books—Adam Motin, in particular—for getting behind this book; Kevin Castro, for getting this project off the ground; and all of the wrestlers and talent who contributed to this project.

—Jimmy "Superfly" Snuka and Jon Chattman

I knew I had a lot to say when I began to work on this book, but I have a hard time explaining myself and finding the right words. I didn't stay in school; I wanted to be outside with nature. I had confidence when it came to sports but not in the classroom. Since I wasn't good in school, I didn't want to go.

Writing this book made me realize how much work it takes to do it right, and this book would not exist without my dear brudda Jon Chattman. He took control and kept me on track. I first met Jon in 2009 when he was writing his book, *A Battle Royal in the Sky*. He wanted to interview me for his book, and we talked for a little bit. I liked him right away. He was very friendly and very professional, and he just knew the right questions to ask. I do so many interviews and people always ask me the same questions. Brudda Jon was different. When the chance came about to work with Jon again, I knew he was the right writer.

Jon is a new dad; his son, Noah, was born just a few weeks before we started working on the book. I need to thank Alison, Jon's wife, for allowing me to take up Jon's time and excusing my late-night texting and emails when I had information I needed to share with him. So, congratulations brudda! I am glad that we are celebrating your first hardcover book—and my first book—together. I am glad to be able to call you my friend and brudda. I love you!

To Sharon—thank you for my beautiful children: Jimmy, Liana, Sarona, and Ata. The two of us were like oil and water, but you raised my kids when I was gone and I thank you for that.

I also want to take this opportunity to thank my fellow wrestlers for looking out for me all these years; we are a team when we get into the ring. When I call you my bruddas, I mean it. You are truly my brothers and sisters. When I am on the road and away from my family, *you* are my family. Thanks for taking time out from your busy schedules to say a few words and share a few stories about the Superfly.

To my children—I love you with all my heart. I was blessed with three beautiful daughters and my main man Jimmy—my son who was the man of the house when I was away. Thank you for looking after your mother and sisters for me. Thanks to my daughter Liana, who was my secretary and kept me up to date while I was away; my daughter Sarona, who I called Paki' because of her beautiful eyes; and my youngest daughter Ata, who I call Curly because of her beautiful curly hair. My job took me away from home often and I missed many birthdays, ballgames, holidays, and special events. I loved my work, and you all made it possible for me to do it. Every time I enter the ring, I know you are with me, and I give you my special sign so you know Dad is thinking about you. Without your love and understanding, I would not have been able to accomplish these things in my life.

Thank you to my brother, Henry, for helping me to remember dates and places. Sorry I got you into trouble back when we were kids, but we did have fun! Thank you to my sisters Louise and Vicky, who brought back so many memories for me. You will always be my little sisters.

To all my family from around the world—Fiji, Australia, New Zealand, the Marshall Islands, and the Gilbert Islands—it was great to find you and talk with you about my mother and father. You have filled in so many blanks for me, and I feel so much closer to you all. You are my family and I love you.

Finally, I want to thank my lovely wife, Carole. When I met you, I was at a low point in my life. I was getting divorced and did not get to see my family very often. I thought my life was over, but you helped me see that I had a lot of life left to live. You never gave up on me. You helped me get my health back and gave me a stable family life. I love our little shack and my lawn. You are my best friend and I love spending my days and night with you. Thank you for talking me into writing this book.

—Jimmy "Superfly" Snuka

I would like to thank Jimmy "Superfly" Snuka for being so honest, kind, and open during this entire process. Jimmy has lived an amazing life in and out of the ring, and I'm so appreciative that he allowed me into his world. Just as he's been his entire life, Jimmy was fearless when it came to telling his story. He never held back, no matter how personal the questions got during the writing process, and no matter how hurtful it was to relive some of the tragedies in his life. Jimmy would always tell Carole and me that this book had to be the truth, and because of that mind-set, this book is an honest, fearless portrayal of a true icon. Jimmy, I loved you as a wrestler growing up, and now I can say I love you as a person, brudda! I'm honored to call you a friend, and I hope one day I can be on the receiving end of one of your signature splashes!

I would especially like to thank Carole for helping out tremendously in putting this book together. I thank her for her devotion to Jimmy and her dedication to making this book the best it could be. Her additional research helped make this book what it is. I'd also like to thank her for filming some of those promos of Jimmy and me. Watch your back, Meryl Streep!

I would also like to thank all the Snuka, Maston, Thomas, and Reiher family members whom I had the pleasure of speaking with or who helped Carole with the book—Louise, Henry, Sarona, Liana, Jimmy Jr., Ata, Rich, and Bridget. They all shared stories about Jimmy and gave me great insight into his life outside the ring. I can never thank them enough for answering my often deeply personal questions with class and dignity.

Thanks to Adam Motin of Triumph Books for bringing this project my way in the fall of 2011. It has been a truly amazing experience working with Triumph on this book, as well as *I Love the Red Sox/I Hate the Yankees*. I hope this partnership continues in the future. I'd also like to thank Kevin Castro for his involvement and dedication to capturing the Superfly's legacy, and for introducing me to the Snukas. I am truly grateful for his help.

I'd especially like to thank all of the wrestling talent and industry professionals who took the time to speak with me and share stories on the Superfly, no matter how hectic their schedules were. I grew up idolizing some of them, and to speak with them directly and gain their insight into a business I loved was a wonderful experience. I wouldn't want to omit anyone, so I will list all of the talent who spoke with me about Jimmy: Dwayne "The Rock" Johnson, Ricky "The Dragon" Steamboat, Rocky Johnson, Bob Backlund, Gerald Brisco, Matt Borne, Mean Gene Okerlund, Rob Van Dam, Jeff Hardy, Jeff "Metal Maniac" Miller, The Iron Sheik, Don Muraco, Paul Orndorff, Tito Santana, Shane Helms, Tom Brandi, Nikolai Volkoff, Dave Meltzer, Bill Apter, Lanny Poffo, Terry Funk, Kurt Angle, and Dawn Marie. I'd like to send special thanks to Ata Maivia Johnson for her assistance throughout the project.

I'd like to single out three wrestlers, in particular, for going the extra mile for Jimmy and this book. Mick Foley and Rowdy Roddy Piper—thank you for sharing your personal stories in your introduction and foreword, respectively. Your opening remarks gave context to the man Jimmy is and the legacy he has left this industry. I'd also like to thank Tommy Dreamer for his comments on the Superfly and for also getting the word out about this book to his friends in the business. In brief, I would also like to thank the following people for their involvement: Greg Casterioto, Andy Vineberg, Shane Victorino, Billy Corgan, Evan Ginzburg, Lewis Kay, Todd Brodginski, Barbara Goodish, Clark Gregg, Judah Friedlander, Constantine Maroulis, Sal Iacono, Questlove, Sam Roberts, and Frankie DeFalco.

There are many people in my life who have supported me throughout my whole career. I would personally like to thank my good friend and wrestling guru John Miele for his endless support and assistance from day one on the "Snuka booka," and for his assistance in making sure I got all the facts straight. Words can't describe how grateful I am to him for that. I should also thank his wife, Karen, for letting him spend so much time helping me out—especially considering they were planning their wedding! Thanks to friends Andrew Plotkin, Rich Tarantino, and Allie and Shira Tarantino, in particular, for their loyalty and support for this book and pretty much everything else I've ever worked on. I value your friendship more than you could know. Thanks, in particular, to Rich for getting me involved with Triumph Books and for the EEW payday I know will likely come one day soon...I hope, anyway. Thanks to longtime friends Alyson Tina and Keith Troy for their friendship and loyalty. Loyalty means everything to me, and it's hard to find friends as loyal as you.

I'm grateful to my family—they have provided me with such a strong support system and continue to inspire me. Thanks to my wife, Alison, for her love and patience during this entire process. I worked really hard on this book, and I know it couldn't have been easy for her to have my nose in my laptop or my ear to my cell phone so often—especially considering I started this book two weeks after our son, Noah, was born. Thank you for helping me balance changing diapers with writing Snuka chapters. It's also important for me to thank my mother-in-law, aka Nana, for pitching in so much and making this new part of our lives easier. I am eternally grateful. Thanks to my parents Gary and Patti, aka Grandpa and Nana, for all your endless love (and no, that has nothing to do with Lionel Richie or Diana Ross). Thanks to my mom for giving me such a strong foundation as a child. Thanks for the Herman funeral, and the trip to NYC to face my fears and watch *Gremlins* from start to finish. I love you.

Thanks to my father for taking me to all those wrestling shows back in the day, and thanks to my mom for buying me plenty of WWF action figures—the rubbery ones—as well as the WWF ice cream bars (I ate too many of the latter). I want to thank my sister, Alissa, her husband, Jake, and my nephew, Ryan, for their support. I wonder if Ryan will throw a Nitro party when he's older.

Last and far from least—this book is for my son, Noah. I love you so very much, and even though you've only been a part of my life for a short time, I cannot remember what life was like before you. My life really started the day you were born. I hope one day to take you to wrestling events, just as my dad took me. This book, and anything I do, I dedicate to you. I love you, monkey!

—Jon Chattman